VOLUME THREE

LADIES *of*
GOLD

THE REMARKABLE MINISTRY OF THE GOLDEN CANDLESTICK

The Authorized Compilation by
JAMES MALONEY

WESTBOW
PRESS
A DIVISION OF THOMAS NELSON

WestBow Press books may be ordered through booksellers or by contacting:

WestBow Press
A Division of Thomas Nelson
1663 Liberty Drive
Bloomington, IN 47403
www.westbowpress.com
1-(866) 928-1240

ISBN: 978-1-4497-5357-3 (sc)
ISBN: 978-1-4497-5359-7 (hc)
ISBN: 978-1-4497-5358-0 (e)

Library of Congress Control Number: 2012909239

Printed in the United States of America

WestBow Press rev. date: 05/23/2012

CONTENTS

THE LAST (FORE)WORD

We've now arrived at the last installment of the collected works of the Golden Candlestick. Thanks for taking the time to read these writings; I hope they're inspiring, and that the Lord uses them to draw you nearer to Himself. As I wrote in the last installment, if you haven't read Volumes One and Two yet, may I suggest you do so before diving into this last book.

I've spent the previous two forewords sort of gently cautioning the reader to submit what they're reading here to the Lord for a divine revelation of just what the GC was all about. Not because it's errant—far from it! But bottom line is most of us have never heard of the kind of rapture and translation experiences Frances Metcalfe considered regular occurrences. Until recently, they've not been very widely discussed topics in the charismatic Body—we usually think of *rapture* as "THE" rapture, some time in the future, perhaps envisioning Kirk Cameron as the leader of those Left Behind. (That's probably trademarked.)

This last installment is focused more on the Lord and His relationship to the Bride; how we as the Bride are expected to prepare ourselves for that glorious day when we meet our Bridegroom in the air. (And Kirk Cameron will be there, don't worry.) The following material might be a little less "sensational" than the first two volumes, and I don't think that's a bad thing. The whole point of Frances' ministry was to drive the Bride into the Lord's embrace with reckless abandon, with undying fervor, with passionate focus. The intent of any rapture/translation experience was to further that singular goal: "That I might know Him." I want to reemphasize that here, just to make sure we're clear on why we're putting out books of this nature.

I think it's great we're seeking the glory encounters, the supernatural manifestations of God's awesomeness and might; but the only legitimate, lasting way into those encounters is by seeking Him, just for Himself, because He alone is worthy; not just what He's willing to do for us in the name of signs and wonders. And this is coming from a person the Lord has deigned to use as a prophetic healing minister. Every one of the books we've put out has been about glory encounters, signs, wonders, miracles, healings, deliverances, radical salvations—all to point you to seek the Lord solely for who He is. Worship Him, and then you don't have to worry about whether or not we're all raptured or translated twenty times before breakfast.

So that's why I think it's fitting we end this *Ladies of Gold* series on this kind of note. Let's describe the King, and His Queen (that's us), and let's hopefully offer a few tidbits on how to prepare ourselves for that glorious Day of the Lord. I can't wait for His appearing! Can you?

Now, lastly, I've got a surprise for you dear readers. We have Frances' journal on the "First Missionary Journey" of the Golden Candlestick. It's a diary of her account to Israel and other countries. We were going to include it in Volumes 2 and 3, but when we started transcribing it, we realized it would be too large to include in these books—making them too expensive. So, we're going to put it out as a separate book. It's not really part of the GC's "collected works," in the strictest sense of the words, but it does give some insight into Frances and what she was all about. There's some unique thoughts, a little teaching, and generally just an interesting story. We'll probably put it out later this year—keep an eye out for it.

In the meantime, enjoy the *Ladies of Gold*. Thanks again for taking the time to read it. I trust the Lord that His Spirit will bless you as you go through it.

—James Maloney
February 1, 2012
Argyle, Texas

THE KING'S PORTRAIT

Frances Metcalfe

INTRODUCTION

An amazingly composite and complete portrait of Jesus Christ, the King of Kings, was painted five hundred years before His actual birth! The artist who portrayed Him with such superb skill beheld this glorious King and His coming Kingdom in a series of heavenly visions. To him was given angelic assistance, that he might make known unto Judah—and, eventually, to the entire world—the Messiah's power, holiness, beauty, and surpassing glory. The "oil" he utilized for this portrait was the anointing oil of the Holy Spirit; his brush was the Word of God; the canvas, of course, was the parchment upon which God's irradiant words were inscribed.

The ravages of time have destroyed many a masterpiece of ancient art. But this one, praise God! has been wondrously preserved. And doubtless each of us has at least one copy of it in our possession. Yet, because it is so readily accessible, it is possible that we have never really contemplated it and appreciated it as we should. At least we—of The Golden Candlestick Company—found this to be the case, when the Holy Spirit held it before our dazzled eyes week after week, and impressed us to scrutinize it minutely. What a marvelous new revelation of Jesus Christ and His Kingdom dawned upon our illumined hearts and minds as we did so!

As a result of this revelation, we have been prompted by the Spirit to share our experience, and to offer this portrait of the King anew to you at this hour when the world is undergoing chaotic upheavals in preparation for His coming and setting up of His

Kingdom. If you have thrilled and responded to Christ as King, and to "the message of the Kingdom," you are sure to find joy in this presentation. We must of necessity condense our words and limit the size of this book. But the Holy Spirit can so expand and enhance our testimony that you could be swept into a more glorious vision of the King and the Kingdom than you have hitherto experienced. Oh may it be so!

INTRODUCING THE ARTIST

We shall appreciate The King's Portrait more fully if we are first introduced to the artist who gave it to the world, and learn to know him in a personal way. Zechariah, "The Prophet of the Messiah," is truly worthy of a special place in our hearts.

Among the books of the twelve minor prophets, he shines out like a brilliant morning star, heralding the passing of the night and the dawn of the daystar, the radiant Son of God. Not only does he portray Christ's first coming, but also His great latter-day appearing and world-wide Kingdom. His words, which spoke dynamically to God's remnant in his own day, speak with even greater authority to us in our day. His book has been appropriately named, "The Apocalypse of the Testament." Martin Luther highly prized it and called it "the model, pattern and quintessence of all prophecy." Yet it has often been overlooked or neglected—as have the other "minor prophets." The Jews found this book most puzzling, since they were blind to the true Messiah. And even many of the early fathers considered it difficult to interpret. How thrilling it is to us, therefore, that the Holy Spirit has faithfully illuminated it to us for many years, and has recently quickened and impressed it upon our hearts in a new way.

Concerning Zechariah there is not much revealed in the Scriptures, even though he is an admirable and fascinating figure in

God's Word. It is known that his father, Berechiah, and grandfather, Iddo, were priests; and that he was likely instructed in Godliness from the time of his youth. He was born in Babylon and returned to Jerusalem with the first remnant. His father seems either to have died or not returned. So he is called the son of Iddo. He seems to have been quite young at the beginning of his office. And we know that he was dedicated to the Lord and was holy in His eyes, "For the prophecy came not in old time by the will of man: but holy men of God spake as they were moved by the Holy Ghost." He was a seer and mystic of unusual sensitivity; yet he was a man of action—he did not shun to speak forth boldly concerning sin. When we put together the meaning of the names recorded here, we find them forming a very precious message. Iddo—*timely;* Berechiah—*one whom God blesses;* Zechariah—*God remembers:* At God's set time He remembers and blesses His people!

It is said that Zechariah lived to be very old and that he prophesied over a long period of time. But only this one book was written and preserved. Tradition records that God worked miracles through him, and that all the people were in awe of him. They said that the spirit of Jeremiah dwelt in him. He seems to have had a most unusual communion with saints and angels. In fact *no other prophet speaks of them as he does.* They played an important role in his ministry. They were active too at the time of Jesus' birth. Again, in The Revelation, John speaks of them continually, and *in the latter days they are to play a great part in the earth.* So it is surely reasonable that one who was so transported into the Latter Days should enjoy such communion and assistance.

Zechariah used visions and symbols to portray truths so great and far-reaching that they could not have been expressed in everyday language. Just as in the Book of The Revelation, the great plan of God is veiled in symbolic language, which cannot be understood unless it is interpreted by the Holy Spirit. The Author alone can reveal the full meaning of this prophecy. Yet, in some cases, the words are simple and direct and had a literal fulfillment. There were limited, local fulfillments in the age in which it was written; there have been (and will be) personal fulfillments in believing hearts throughout the ages; and *there is yet to be a later, universal fulfillment which will expand throughout eternity.* Therefore these visions and symbols, in this vital portrait, and these poetic utterances, are of vital historical, personal and prophetical significance to us.

> The spirit moved upon me
> In a strange and mysterious way:
> It seemed I was transported
> Back to Zechariah's day;
> I walked in old Jerusalem
> By night, as he did then,
> And saw the angels all around
> Encamping there again.
> O Jerusalem! O Jerusalem!
>> Jehovah has set His love on thee.
>> O Jerusalem! O Jerusalem!
>> His angels guard thee faithfully.
>> I seemed to hear the murmur
> Of the gentle evening breeze,
> And my eyes beheld a Man
> Beneath the fragrant myrtle trees.
> I heard Him interceding,
> Jerusalem, for thee;
> And in answer to His pleading
> God spoke most graciously.
> O Jerusalem! O Jerusalem!
>> I, the Lord, am jealous over thee.
>> O Jerusalem! O Jerusalem!

Thine enemies I'll vanquish utterly.
As I pondered on this wonder,
Oh, much to my surprise,
A candlestick made all of gold
Appeared before my eyes!
Two olive trees were flourishing,
One upon each side,
Pouring forth their golden oil
To keep her lamps supplied.
O Jerusalem! O Jerusalem!
Thy candlestick has burned throughout the night.
O Jerusalem! O Jerusalem!
The nations soon shall walk in thy light.

CHAPTER ONE

THE MESSIAH AS INTERCESSOR

Zechariah's first recorded vision of the Messiah, the Anointed One, reveals Him as both man and "angel (messenger) of The Lord of Hosts." So vividly did the prophet paint this picture of Him that its colors are as bright today as they were in 520 B.C. But before we fix our eyes upon this portrait, it is imperative that we give careful consideration to the first six verses of this chapter, for these provide the *key* to the entire book. Zechariah was a true prophet of God and herald of the Kingdom. Therefore he began his message and ministry with a stirring call to *repentance* and *return* to the Lord. He did not fear or shun to declare the wrath of the Lord against sin and unbelief. It has been said that he gave the strongest call to repentance in the Old Testament, and one can readily feel in it the same authority and unction with which John the Baptist later called Israel to repentance and prepared their hearts for the actual physical coming of the Messiah.

Had not Judah listened to Zechariah, and repented and turned the Lord, all the promises and revelations later given through him would have been withheld. Likewise, it is true in our day that those who desire to behold the Lord and experience the glories of His Kingdom must first follow the way of thorough repentance and return to the God of the Bible. We live in an age of appeasement and fraternization with evil, and many of the would-be prophets and ministers of Christ have banished all preaching of the *wrath* of God—His *indignation against* and *certain judgment* of evil, both in His church and in the world. False Kingdom messengers, they!

Not so Zechariah! His vital concern was for the spiritual purity and moral integrity of Judah. Pure walk, pure worship! Blessed, oh blessed indeed, are the pure in heart, for they shall *see* God. And Zechariah did!

"I had been viewing the night, and lo! There appeared a man mounted on a red horse. He stood among the myrtle trees which are in the valley (Kidron)." (Verse 8) This Man was none other than the Messiah, preparing to ride forth against the nations who had been cruelly afflicting Israel. Red here typifies fiery judgment. This mysterious "man" is also referred to as the Angel of the LORD. (Christ appeared as such in other Old Testament theophanies also.) How beautifully both the human and divine nature of Jesus are thus combined in this composite picture! The myrtle was a symbol of Judah. Its fragrant white blossoms are most bridal and it loves to grow in low, well watered places. Esther's Jewish name, Hadassah, means myrtle. And Isaiah says that the myrtle is "an everlasting sign." (Isaiah 55:13)

The Jew, as we know, is indeed an everlasting sign which shall not be cut off. But so too is the Church, the Bride of Christ, and her sons are for "signs and wonders." Just as the Messiah appeared to vanquish the enemies of Judah (and did, in the following years), so shall He appear among His Bride and vanquish the latter day enemies of The Church.

Our prophet, who has boldly declared the wrath and judgment of Jehovah, now hears the Messiah, as the Angel of the Lord, intercede with the Father and call upon Him for mercy. (Verse 12) The priests were still disputing among themselves about when the appointed seventy years of captivity would end exactly. But the Messiah knew the Father's timing to the moment, "and called upon Him to intervene and to show mercy and favor unto His remnant. Christ is indeed the *great Intercessor,* the *Vessel of Mercy* unto every age. And the ministry of intercession which He continues at the Father's right hand is a vital necessity for the deliverance and preservation of His people. Likewise, through the agency of the Holy Spirit, intercession is being poured out by the Body of Christ on earth. It is evident that the *ministry of the Intercessor is always required to bring God's mercy and power into the world.*

Suddenly, before our entranced eyes, this portrait of the Messiah seems to be set ablaze with divine jealousy—a word in the Hebrew sometimes translated as "the very flame of YHVH." The great eternal love of the Lord for Jerusalem and Israel is indeed a consuming fire. (Verse 14) As a faithful Lover and Husband, the Lord thus returned to Israel. His House, He declared, would be built in their midst. (It was!) His prosperity would be spread abroad throughout her cities. (This too came to pass!) He promised to comfort and bless her, and protect her against all her enemies. (And He kept His word!) Mercy gloried over judgment, just as it does in this Latter Day when Jesus Christ appears in our midst, too, as the MAN who rides forth in judgment upon Communism and all other enemies of His Spiritual Israel; when He and His consecrated priests pour out intercession, and when His love and divine jealousy flame forth in consuming fire. So he appeared to Zechariah, and so too, praise God! He has appeared unto us.

ZECHARIAH

Zechariah, Zechariah,
Priest and Prophet of the Lord.
Once again we hear your call,
As we read your word.
And we feel your holy zeal
For the Lord of Hosts
To bring again His Zion people
Back from foreign coasts.

Zechariah, we would help you
Build the Temple of the Lord,
Until our King and true Messiah
Comes, fulfilling all your word.

—Marian Pickard

CHAPTER TWO

THE MESSIAH AS THE BUILDER

Before Jerusalem could be rebuilt and the Temple of God completed, the Lord, the Master Builder, must survey the City and prepare to lay the foundations according to the divine Blueprint. In a vision He appears therefore to Zechariah again as a man, and now he is holding a measuring line in His hand, preparing to make this survey. (Also unto Ezekiel the Lord appeared in this form [Chap. 40], and again in Revelation 11:1 we find that John was given a measuring reed and was commanded to measure the Temple of God, the Altar, and "them that worship therein.") In less than one hundred years after this vision, a literal man did come and survey the city and plan to rebuild the walls. This man, of course, was Nehemiah.

There is much instruction in God's Word about measurements. Just as God perfectly *times* His works, so too does He accurately *measure* them. In the building of the Tabernacle and the Temple specific measurements were given for each detail. These were *literally* carried out according to the "blueprint" God gave His servants. But they also had numerically symbolical significance. God is an expert mathematician, and everything in nature verifies this fully as the Scriptures. Job tells us that He weighs the winds and measures the waters. (Job 28:25) He also marvelously balances

17

the clouds by careful measure. (Job 37:16) And He stretched forth a measuring line when He laid the foundations of the earth. (Job 38:5,6) And again He shall measure the earth. (Hab. 3:6) The wisdom of God shown in the measurements and weights of the material universe is a wonder to all sincere students of science. And in our own physical bodies can be found the greatest wonders of all. Not only are the hairs of our heads numbered, but also the atoms of our structure and even the chromosomes in each cell nucleus.

How often the Spirit has impressed us that *God is weighing us in the balances and measuring us for His eternal purposes.* Our Lord made it plain that whatever measure we mete shall determine the measure meted to us. Grace bestows God's power and favor abundantly. But *we receive only the measure for which we have faith and capacity.* It is clear that Kingdom privileges and glory can be given to us only as we measure up to God's standard—His blueprint for sonship. Jerusalem is measured. Zion is measured. We, His worshipers, are measured. We must be fitted perfectly into God's eternal City and Temple.

The Man with the measuring line fades from view, and again the Husband and Defender of Israel is revealed. He calls to Zion to return from Babylon and find her safety in the City He shall build. He will be a wall of fire round about her, and a glory in her midst. He will protect her as the apple of His eye, and will personally dwell in the midst of her. How often He tried to teach Israel that He was their only Defender! But always they turned to human means of warfare and strength. Just as we do today! Our nation says, "In God we Trust." But we madly vie with other nations in our armament race. In our own personal lives we tend to erect walls and barriers, behind which we hide from others and seek to escape the pain of open encounters in life's inevitable conflict. The Spirit seeks to break down these walls, and to enlarge us too, to make room for much increase. Denominational walls may be represented here also. The New Testament Church, "Jerusalem," is divided into a series of walled sections. But when Christ comes again these denominational walls must fall. There shall be no more divisions. Already the Spirit has leveled these walls in many of us. Praise God!

This prophecy had only a temporary fulfillment in Zechariah's day. It pointed of course to a far greater increase to come. Veiled behind the little local Jerusalem was the great New Jerusalem which shall indeed be unwalled and most extensive. About 73 years after this, Nehemiah mourned in Shushan about the still unbuilt walls. (Neh. 1) He soon obtained permission from the king to return and lead in the rebuilding. Daniel had prophesied this too. (Dan. 9:25) The building of these walls was doubtless permitted of God, because the Jews were not yet able to fully believe God. Yet it was the walls and fortifications of the City that, centuries later, caused such widespread destruction, when their enemies were again permitted to inflict God's judgments upon them. Had the city been undefended, they might have allowed the Temple and buildings to stand. In World War I, under General Allenby's noble command, Jerusalem was defended as by "birds flying" (British airplanes.) Thus was fulfilled Isaiah's amazing word. (Isa. 31:5) In our day there are no walls high enough and strong enough to protect Jerusalem or any other city! The full meaning of this prophecy will be fulfilled only in the New Jerusalem, and in the spiritual Jerusalem, the City of God.

How often we too have heard the call to arise and flee from Babylon! There is no time for delay. The Lord wants to spare His elect in this day, just as He did then. But He did not supernaturally deliver them from Babylon. They had to rise and act upon His Word. It was required of them—and of us—that they leave behind the Babylonish world system and its ways, both in the commercial and religious worlds. When we obey and take the way of separation unto the Lord, we experience His personal love and blessing in a special way, just as they did. Yes, we are kept even as "the apple of His eye." We too hear the Spirit calling us, singing in us: "Sing and rejoice,

O daughter of Zion: for, lo, I come, and I will dwell in the midst of thee, saith the Lord."

How beautiful is the vision of The Messiah dwelling in joyful communion with Zion, in the Holy Land and Jerusalem, as painted by Zechariah at the close of this chapter. Many nations are gathered there with them, and so awe-inspiring is the presence and power of the Lord that he cries out, "Be silent, oh all flesh, before the Lord: for He is raised up out of His holy habitation." This great gathering of nations never took place in the history of the Jews! Obviously this is a Latter Day prophecy, and refers to His spiritual Zion as well as to His literal Israel, to whom now the remnant are returning out of many nations. When our glorious Lord shall appear and take up His abode in our midst, in an open way, the nations shall indeed be struck with awe and shall turn their hearts unto Him.

REJOICE GREATLY, O ZION

Rejoice greatly, O Zion,
Rejoice and shout and sing!
Behold thy King is come to thee;
Loud let His praises ring.
He is just and very lowly;
Clothed by God the Most Holy,
Rejoice, O daughter Zion,
Thy King comes to thee.

Rejoice greatly, O Zion,
Rejoice and shout and sing!
Thy King shall reign from sea to sea,
And great shall be the victory.
He shall arm thy sons, O Zion,
They shall war like Judah's Lion;

Rejoice, O daughter Zion,
Thy King comes to thee!

—Isabelle Hosking

CHAPTER THREE

THE MESSIAH, THE BRANCH OF JEHOVAH

As the unveiling of the King's composite portrait continues, Zechariah next paints a court scene before our eyes. Joshua, the High Priest of Israel, is on trial before the tribunal of God. As the defendant, he represents all Israel. The accuser, or prosecutor: is none other than Satan himself! Surely this vision must have been shocking to Zechariah, when he first beheld it. To Israel, the High Priest represented their very salvation, for it was he, and only he, who could approach the presence of the Most High God on the Day of Atonement and receive assurance from God that the sins of the nation were forgiven and covered. He was the unique mediator between the Lord and the people. To behold him standing thus in jeopardy, being withstood by so powerful an adversary, must have been a fearful thing to the prophet. (In Job and The Revelation the devil is also shown in this capacity.) But Joshua had an Advocate who was more powerful than his adversary—even the Messiah, Jesus Christ! (1 John 2:1) It is He who rebuked Satan and defended Jerusalem and Joshua. Here is an amazing scene in which the Judge becomes the Advocate, and mercy again glories over judgment! Joshua (Israel), a brand plucked out of the fires of God's judgment, is clothed in filthy garments, as he stands before the Lord. In spite of the ceremonial care with which he had been cleansed, consecrated and clothed, his righteousness is as filthy rags in the presence of

21

the All-Holy. Doubtless, in this vision, the Holy Spirit was revealing the contrast between the Old Testament righteousness, which was only typical and ceremonial, and the perfect righteousness of the Great High Priest to come, Jesus Christ, toward whom all the Old Testament sacrifices and ceremonies pointed. The book of Hebrews throws a revealing light upon this chapter of Zechariah, and we readily understand that it is only Christ who can place upon Joshua, or any of His priests, the pure white garments of his righteousness. It is He who now commands: "Take away the filthy garments from him!" And to Joshua He says, "Behold, I have caused thine iniquity to pass from thee, and I will clothe thee with a change of raiment."

An instantaneous work of grace was then wrought before the eyes of Zechariah, and he was quick to call for the crown or miter (of the High Priest) to be placed upon his head. (Ex. 28:36-39) As we look now upon Joshua, we behold not him, but Jesus Christ, the eternal High Priest, after the "order of Melchizedek." (Psalm 110:4; Heb. 7:21) And in this portrait of Him, as High Priest, we see too a great composite company of Melchizedek priests, who, like Joshua, bear the name of JESUS (it being an Old Testament form of His name), and are clothed with His righteousness. We, who are called to participate in this eternal priesthood, also experience the wrath and scorn of the accuser, and rejoice in the power of our great Advocate. And the words spoken to Joshua are spoken by the Spirit unto us, in this latter day, as we are being prepared for this royal priesthood: "If thou wilt walk in my ways, and if thou wilt keep my charge, then thou shalt also judge my house, and shalt also keep my courts, and I will give thee places to walk among these that stand by."

How true it is that all the Kingdom promises and blessings of the Lord are *conditional;* and their individual fulfillment is dependent upon the faith and obedience of the "sons of the Kingdom." The great "IF" is always the equivocal factor. Up to this point, Joshua had been protected, delivered, clothed and crowned by GRACE, through the mediation of the Messiah. But now *his cooperation with the grace of God* is called for, and he is strictly charged about his walk and his ways before the Lord. It is only the *doers* of the Word who shall inherit the glories and blessings of the Kingdom! And today, as in Zechariah's day, the Lord's threefold promises to His priests are being fulfilled. If they keep His charge: 1) They are placed in ruling positions in God's House, His spiritual Temple; 2) they lead God's people in the worship and in the ways of the Spirit; 3) the heavenly sanctuary of the Lord is opened to them, and they are brought into communion with saints and angels, as they are taken into the fellowship of the General Assembly on high. (Heb. 12:22-24) These privileges are not given as an instantaneous gift of grace—as were the raiment and the crown—but are bestowed as we walk daily in progressive obedience and union with our Great High Priest.

This special revelation about the communion of saints and angels is most precious, because so little mention is made of this in the Old Testament. In these days the Holy Spirit is bringing many of God's sons into this communion. One translation reads here: "I will give you angel helpers." And He does! The original text here is clear: Joshua would have open access to the presence of the Lord and to the heavenly hosts. And, wonder of wonders! beyond all this, the Lord promises, "I will bring forth my servant the BRANCH." The Hebrew word used here is "tsehmakh," meaning sprout, branch or spring. This word is used also in Isaiah and Jeremiah, and always refers to THE MESSIAH. Sometimes it is translated, "the day-spring." It was also revealed that Joshua and his fellow priests would be "wonders" or "signs"—just as Jesus said His sons would be. (Heb. 2:13)

A mysterious jewel is also placed before the eyes of Joshua. It has seven eyes, or facets, and reminds us at once of Christ, the Lamb, in Revelation 5:6. Christ, the suffering Servant, the Lamb of God, is the foundation stone of Zion. (Isa. 28:16) "And," says the Lord, "I will remove the iniquity of the land in one day." Centuries later, on that "one day," that unique and great day that was the most momentous day the world has ever seen, Jesus Christ, the Messiah, bore the sins of the world in His own body on the Cross. He tasted death for every man, and by one offering atoned for and provided for the complete righteousness of all who would accept His vicarious sacrifice. How wonderful it is that Zechariah portrayed all of this in his portrait of the King more than 500 years before Jesus was born into the world!

CHAPTER FOUR

THE MESSIAH, THE LIGHT OF THE WORLD

One of the titles we delight to give Jesus is "The Light of the World." And artists, in all generations, have attempted to portray the supernal light and glory that is the very essence of His being. When the prophet Simeon actually held the Christ Child in his arms and looked into His beautiful face, he cried out: "A light to lighten the Gentiles (nations) and the glory of thy people Israel." To Zechariah the Messiah, as the Light of Israel, was revealed in the form of a most marvelous golden candlestick, and he painted the vision of what he saw most vividly. As we read it, we are at once reminded of John's even more glorious vision of the Risen Christ walking in the midst of the seven golden candlesticks. To any Hebrew, the symbol of the Candlestick, or Menorah, was immediately understood to stand for the Word, the Testimony of Jehovah. And to this day the menorah is displayed in every Jewish synagogue.

The candlestick described in Exodus 25 was a special article of worship placed in the Holy Place of the Tabernacle, to illuminate it and the Table of Show bread and Altar of Incense. Its light was provided by a specially prepared, pure olive oil, which the priests provided and poured into it, day and night, so that its light would never be extinguished. The pure gold of it represented the purity and divinity of Christ, the "true and faithful witness," the "incarnate Testimony or Word of the Father." The beaten work and beaten oil depicted his sufferings. The lamps were seven—indicating the seven-fold Spirit of God. The almond-shape bowls on the branches, and the flowers engraved on it, depicted the budding of Aaron's rod and the grace and beauty of eternal life and light.

Zechariah must have known also about another Candlestick which at certain periods of time was used in Israel during the Feast of Tabernacles. This one was very large, perhaps as tall as 35 feet. It was placed in the Court of the Women during the Feast, and its light was visible throughout the City of Jerusalem. Since in The Revelation, Jesus Himself says that the Candlesticks are His churches, and while on earth He likened His disciples to a light that was put on a candlestick, and a city that could not be hidden, we can readily see in Zechariah's beautiful Candlestick that both the Messiah and His Body, His Church, were being portrayed.

The two olive trees remind us also of the two witnesses spoken of in The Revelation. Some believe that they symbolize the Old and the New Testaments and the anointed "sons" of each Covenant. In any case, the Candlestick Zechariah saw was not the same as the one in Exodus. It is fed by only *one* bowl, placed on the top of it, rather than by seven small bowls. Christ, in His incarnation came forth from one "vessel"—the womb of the Virgin Mary. His church shall be brought forth by a unified Zion—the Mother from Above—and the Holy Spirit shall illumine the world through Christ and manifest in His church. And they shall be one, as He and the Father are one.

The words of the angel to Zechariah, in answer to his question about the two olive trees, is one of the most precious portions of the Old Testament: "Not by (human) might, nor by (human) power, but by my Spirit, saith the Lord of Hosts." How often this Word has been sounded forth in these latter days! It has become a battle cry for the Spirit-filled hosts of the Lord. Yet often the equally important next words of the angel are overlooked: "Who art thou, O great mountain? Before Zerubbabel thou shalt become a plain: And he shall bring forth the *headstone* thereof with shoutings, crying 'Grace, grace unto it.'" The great mountain referred to Babylon, and all earthly and satanic power that might be rallied against Judah. Zerubbabel, the Davidic representative who was to finish the Temple, was commanded to exercise mountain-moving faith, depending on the Spirit and the GRACE of God. Just as they had shouted when the foundations had been laid (Ezra 3:11-13), so would they shout when the Temple was completed. Think how radical this word was in the days of Zechariah, when the emphasis was placed on the *law* and *ceremonial religion*. Yes, it is by *grace* and by the *Spirit* Zion is to be built, and the Temple of Living Stones will be raised up for the glory of the Lord.

In these latter days we have marveled at the manifestation of the *great grace* of our Lord, and at the increasing outpourings of the Holy Spirit. We too shall see the finished work in the nations accomplished by His might, and by "Grace, grace!" And in Christ we shall be to the praise of the glory of his grace, throughout all eternity. One of the symbolic meanings of Zion is "God's revealed grace." And our illumined eyes have beheld the King, walking in the midst of His golden candlesticks, and full of GRACE and TRUTH.

CORONATION

Zechariah smelted a crown for Him that day,
His Kingdom is an endless one!
He shall be crowned in that golden day and
They shall proclaim Him Heir—God's only Son!

A coronet of the precious ore
The captives brought from Babylon;
Though the witnesses wore it,
It was for the King of Kings—God's Holy One!

—Norma Lamb

CHAPTER FIVE

THE MESSIAH, THE WORD OF JUDGMENT

As Zechariah's heavenly visions continued, His portrait of the King became increasingly kaleidoscopic. In his eighth vision he saw the Messiah as the Word of Judgment. The scene is a dark one, contrasting strongly with the glorious light of the Golden Candlestick. Holy light makes manifest the works of darkness and inevitably brings them into judgment. In the Scriptures, a roll or scroll depicts The Word of God. When Zechariah beheld this large flying scroll, he carefully noted its *position*, its *size*, its *message* and its *fulfillment*.

Positionally, it was flying as though on wings—a symbol sometimes used in referring to angels. And the Covenant of the Law had been mediated by angels unto Moses, as we recall. The Jews believed that when God *spoke* a word, it might later be altered somewhat or mitigated through changing circumstances; but when a Word was *written,* it could never be changed or set aside. We are living in a day when the Spirit speaks frequently through His anointed servants. And we too have learned that such prophecies are conditional and sometimes subject to change. Hence, we test all things by the written Word of the Lord the Word that has stood the test of the centuries. We believe that it is still the most perfect form of TRUTH given to man in spite of the inevitable changes in translation into many languages, except for Jesus Christ, Himself, the Living Word who IS TRUTH. The scroll the prophet saw was obviously *open,* for had this not been the case, Zechariah could not have seen its size so clearly. The *size* of the scroll was significant also. We have learned that God's measurements are most meaningful. So it interests us, as doubtless it did Zechariah, that the dimensions are exactly those of Solomon's porch in the Temple. It was from this porch that the law was often read to the people. It also fits those of the Tabernacle in the wilderness.

The *message* of the scroll was a "curse" or judgment. The Hebrew root means "to adjure or swear." God's curse is never to be confused with man's curse, which is usually "qalal" in the Scriptures, and means to revile, hate, afflict or bring into contempt. Man curses from an evil, destructive heart. The Lord, on the other hand, never curses His people in hatred or from a desire for revenge or punishment. He does—and indeed must—adjure and renounce evil. But His curse is designed to be remedial rather than merely punitive. The cursing of the fig tree (Judah), by our Lord, was an open sign of the withering which was to come to Judah as a result of their own unbelief and self-will. From the beginning the Lord had set before Israel both blessing and cursing. (Deut. 27) The curse of the Lord is actually the *negative* aspect of His *blessing*—the loving favor and grace which has been rejected and forfeited.

Our Lord warned us that every branch in Him that does not bear fruit shall be cut away and burned. (John 18:1-8) Thus we learn that God's curse inevitably follows sin and disobedience. Yet it is always designed to bring man into repentance and restoration. What joy it gives us to know that Christ has fully and completely redeemed our souls from the curse of the Law. (Gal. 3:13) However, in spite of this, our branches may be fruitless; our works may have to be destroyed as wood, hay and stubble, if we prove unfaithful and persist in unbelief. If we are thus guilty, we too will rob the Lord of His portion and glory in us, just as Israel was accused of stealing, according to this scroll. We too shall be guilty of false swearing and irreverence if we have not revered and obeyed Him as we should. In fact, the Holy Spirit has made it plain to us, from time to time, that we have often robbed God of *time, praise, glory* and *love,* as well as of tithes and offerings. (Mal. 3:8,9) Each time we allow doubt, fear, unbelief or self-love to motivate us, we rob God to some extent. We also rob the entire Body of Christ, for our prayers are always hindered by such defeats and losses. And in addition to robbing the Lord directly, we rob one another by withholding good and blessing that is in our power to bestow when we fail to pray for others and minister to their needs. (Prov. 3:27,28) Or we may rob someone of the love and consideration of another, by speaking critically of them, or putting them in the wrong light. The ways in which we can—and sometimes do—rob God and others, are indeed manifold.

The *fulfillment* of the message of the scroll was devastating. Not only was the individual to be cut off, but his house also would be consumed. One translation for "cut off" is "purged or scoured." This offers comfort and hope to the offenders. But consumed is a final word, and again we are reminded of the burning of the unfruitful branches in the Vine, and the destruction of the wood, hay and stubble. Israel was to be thus judged for taking the Lord's name in

29

vain, swearing falsely by Him and failing to keep their vows. That this Word was fulfilled at a later day is certain. Even the Temple itself was destroyed. But in the days of Zechariah, this word of warning was heeded by Israel. and the Lord did manifest grace and mercy unto them. The curse did not come upon them until centuries later.

In Zechariah's ninth vision he beheld a strange sight indeed, a woman hidden in an ephah, a large basket. However astounded he may have been, he faithfully painted this woman into the background of his composite portrait of the King. In the Scriptures, woman is used to typify both good and evil. Mother Zion has an evil counterpart in the harlot Babylon, just as the Son of Man has an evil counterpart in the man of sin. The Lord of Hosts determined to rid Israel of idolatry in every form, and it is a matter of record that after the time of the Captivity, they did not turn again to idols or false religions. Babylon and its unholy ways were soon to be banished from Israel. How readily we see the counterpart of this vision in Revelation 17 and 18. Just as Israel was delivered from the literal Babylon, and all its ways were banished from the Holy Land, so shall the Church of Christ be cleansed and delivered from spiritual Babylon. The literal Babylon, a most marvelous and affluent City and Kingdom was later destroyed and never again restored. We rejoice that soon spiritual Babylon will be completely abolished.

Not only has religious Babylon corrupted all nations, but the spirit of commercial Babylon, based on greed, has permeated every civilized nation. Our own nation is billions of dollars in debt, and yet continues on its drunken orgy of spending and giving away its resources. Our churches are permeated with Babylonish mixtures and materialistic idolatry. The almighty dollar is trusted more than the Almighty God. Our holy days are so permeated with commercialism that they have become a reproach, rather than a blessing.

We too will rejoice when Babylon is removed from our midst. Zechariah, in vision, beheld two women who had wings like the stork, and the wind was in their wings. They lifted up the ephah and bore the evil woman away to the land of Shinar. The stork is a strong migratory bird capable of swift flight. It feeds on snakes and other foul things. And it is believed that in this instance angelic messengers are represented. In any case, wickedness was to be borne away and the land was to be cleansed. A double work of redemption would thus be wrought. In due time, as we know, the curse, pronounced upon all sinners, and especially upon disobedient Israel, the chosen people, was eventually born by Jesus Christ. And in due season His Church and all the earth shall be delivered from all Babylonish works and ways.

Some Prophetic teachers see in this portion of Zechariah's portrait a glimpse of Communism and its latter day power and judgment. Shinar is sometimes translated as China, and the "north country" of course, is said to refer to Russia. It is certain that godlessness and wickedness, blasphemy and lies have found a great "base" or "house" in China, and it has now become the nation which is the greatest threat to world peace. The dragon is its symbol, and this causes us to link Zechariah's visions with those of John recorded in Revelation 12. In this great prophetic book too, as well as in Zechariah's portrait, our Lord is seen as THE WORD OF GOD, manifested in judgment against all evil and victor over all enemies of God.

REJOICE, O ZION

Rejoice, O Zion, be strong and know
The Lord has bent His battle-bow.
And thou art the sword of the Mighty Man;
This hour the evil hosts withstand.

31

His enemies devour and trample down,
For thou art His ensign and His crown.

—Dora Pfnister

[*Incidentally, this is the Dora referred to in* The Dancing Hand of God; *she was, to my knowledge, the last surviving original member of the Golden Candlestick company.* —James Maloney]

CHAPTER SIX

THE MESSIAH, THE CROWNED PRIEST

In bright as well as somber colors, Zechariah continues to paint his background of judgment, including in it now the certain judgment of all nations. In his tenth vision he sees four chariots between mountains of brass. These are obviously angelic agencies. Chariots and horses are usually symbolic of both conquest and judgment. Brass too signifies judgment. The two mountains are thought to be Mount Zion (The King's house) and Mount Moriah (The Temple of the Lord), or Mount of Olives, from whence Jesus ascended and to which He shall return. The Valley of Jehoshaphat lies between. In Joel 3:2, we read: "I will gather all nations, and will bring them down into the Valley of Jehoshaphat, and will plead with them there for my people and for my heritage Israel, whom they have scattered among the nations and *parted my land.* " How perfectly this prophecy in Joel complements Zechariah's portrayal! And how astounding that the partitioning of Palestine was thus foretold. Some interpreters have said that the four great world powers of today are here indicated—the U.S.A., Great Britain, Russia and China. These indeed do head up the nations of the earth and are responsible in a special way. But it is certain that the Lord will deal with all nations.

The black horses, bearing death and sorrow, were to be sent north to Babylon. (About two years after this vision, Darius devastated it because of the rebellion of the Babylonians.) This was a limited, local fulfillment. It is indeed possible that it will have a far greater consummation in the Endtime. Even at this hour China is being weakened by famine and tribulations of a most grievous nature.

The white horses, following the black, could well represent Darius' victory, and could also represent the Lord's eventual victory over the entire Babylonian and Medo-Persian empires. Some versions read that the white horses went *west*. It is certain that the whole movements of Christianity was toward the west, and the great movement of Latter Day messengers and Gospel leaders are now coming from our own country, the most westerly nation from Jerusalem. (Seventy per cent of all Evangelical missionaries and workers are from the U.S.A. according to the latest missionary reports.)

Egypt was usually referred to as "the land to the south." At the time of this prophecy, their relationship with Israel was reasonably peaceful. Throughout the centuries it has varied. It would seem that the Lord's dealings with Egypt have been partly good and partly punitive. For generations it held an obscure place among the nations, except in the eyes of scholars, historians and travelers. However, when Israel returned once more to the Holy Land, Egypt made a sudden comeback! And now, all the world is aware that Egypt is a nation to be reckoned with. The Gaza Strip and the West Bank are daily reminders that ancient prophecy is being revived in the twentieth century.

Sometimes we wonder at the long delay in the accomplishment of the judgments and purposes of the Lord. Violence, injustice and sin abound in our generation on a greater scale than ever before.

Apparently angels are as eager as we to see the earth purged. How often the Holy Spirit has impressed us that the earth must be purged by *blood*—either by the Blood of Christ, or the blood of the victims of the increasingly horrible wars. And now that nuclear war is more than a threat, we long to *see* the great Day of the Lord. And we rejoice to know that His going forth is as certain as the dawn.

Suddenly Zechariah's visions ended and the word of the Lord came to him directly, instructing him to act as well as prophesy. The seer became a doer of the Word! His portrait of the King now becomes animated, much like a motion picture, as we behold the demonstration of God's Word in "living color." Some commentators have said that the portion that begins in Chapter 6 at Verse 10 is the most glorious portrayal of the Messiah in the Old Testament. To the prophet was given the great honor of crowning the Messiah, the great High Priest, in the person of Joshua, his earthly representative. The act was a most unusual one, for the High Priest was not usually thus crowned. It must have been difficult in some ways, for Zechariah to obey this command of the Lord. In Israel the Priesthood and the Ruling line were always separated, and their functions could not be interchanged. To thus place the High Priest in a ruling position would seem to be out of divine order. Yet we who now know Jesus as both King and Priest can readily understand the Truth of the beautiful pageantry enacted by the prophet. It was a drama of the Theocracy of God indeed, for it was not Joshua, but the Messiah, who was thus being honored. Both silver (symbol of redemption) and gold (signifying divinity) were used in the fashioning of the crowns. As this ceremony was carried out, Zechariah was to say: "Thus speaketh the Lord of Hosts, saying, Behold the man whose name is the BRANCH; for he shall grow up out of his place, and he shall build the temple of the Lord: even he shall build the temple of the Lord; and he shall bear the glory, and shall sit and rule upon his throne; and the counsel of peace shall be between them both."

In Chapter Three the Branch was first mentioned, and there He was called, "My servant." Here He is called, "The MAN." The reference to "them both" is puzzling and difficult to explain. Some commentators believe that this was a revelation of the communion of Jesus and the Father, as in the 110th Psalm, "The LORD said unto my Lord..." To Israel the Lord was *one,* and so such references to the Father and Son were veiled and could only be fully understood after the coming of Christ.

It was an unknown thing for the High Priest to be seated upon a throne or indeed upon any kind of seat. No provision was made in the Temple for the priests to sit down at any time. They ministered standing, kneeling or prostrated before the Lord. Rulers and judges are always depicted as seated, executing their authority from a position of rest and security. On the other hand, Jesus is shown also as a Priest in heaven, standing at the right hand of the Father, interceding for His people. Yet He is also going to take His throne and rule, as Zechariah here portrays.

After the dark scenes of judgment and destruction, how inspiring it is to lift up our eyes and behold Jesus Christ, our High Priest and King, crowned and seated upon the throne of God. We are grateful to Zechariah for thus painting Him for us. We thrill too to note a special little side light he has added to the picture: Those whose sacrifice made possible the fashioning of the crowns are to receive them and place them in the temple of the Lord for a memorial. The fame of these men and the crown would spread to other lands, and others too would leave Babylon and come with their loving sacrifices and build the temple. The Holy Spirit thus lovingly encourages those of us who, in this latter day, have left Babylon and brought our sacrifices unto the Lord for the building of the glorious Spiritual House of the Lord. Our substance too can play a blessed part in that building, and our silver (redeemed lives) and gold (purified faith) can be used to crown Him. We too, by His grace, shall be held in everlasting remembrance by the lord, and shall be placed in the great panoramic portrait of the King and His Kingdom.

THE QUEEN'S PORTRAIT

Frances Metcalfe

Upon the King's right hand shall stand
His queen, by prophets long foretold:
Crowned with a royal diadem
And robed with Ophir's finest gold.
Her maidens will be gathered around her,
King's daughters, in splendid array;
And all the nations shall rejoice
To hail her Coronation Day—
The most glorious Bride
Ever to be seen,
Behold, Zion's Queen!

L ike the exquisite painting of an old master, fitly framed in gold, is the portrait of The Queen, etched in the Living Word of God and recorded for us in the last chapter of Proverbs: "The words of King Lemuel, the prophecy that his mother taught him." Some scholars attribute this writing to Solomon, the son of Wisdom, the singer of many royal songs. They believe that he was also called Lemuel, meaning "given of God." And the mother who taught him this song was, of course, Bathsheba. Others say that Lemuel was a king of Massa and that he learned these words from his mother.

It seems more in keeping with the tenor of the Scriptures to attribute this crowning song to Solomon and to place it upon the brow of Bathsheba. Did not the prophet Nathan declare her to be "a ewe lamb"? And did not she, in type, depict the "Ewe," the Bride of the Lamb? He said also of her: "...Whom he has brought and nourished up... it did eat of his own meat (My meat is to do the will of the Father), and drank of his own cup (The cup that I drink, are ye able also to drink of it?), and lay in His bosom (as John did), and was unto him as a daughter." (2 Samuel 12:3) And, again, was it not Bathsheba who obtained the throne for Solomon, and who was given a place at the *right hand* of the king, and was called by him, "The King's Mother"?

Our interest, however, is not focused primarily upon the singer, but upon the song. We are certain that it was inspired by the blessed Holy Spirit of God, and that He with "Mother Wisdom" sang it to us who live in these latter days as surely as to Solomon, or Lemuel, who first captured its beautiful strains. Generation after generation, this song-prophecy has been a favorite theme for preachers, poets and writers. No doubt you have read it, or heard it read, scores of times. Perhaps you have memorized it and cherished its endearing phrases, pondering them in your heart.

When I was a little girl, my mother enjoyed reading it to me. She told me that her mother had taught her that it was the "birthday proverb," and that any woman could find her own birthday verse by taking the one that corresponded to the day of the month on which she was born. Since I was born on the 26th day of the month, I had a very good one indeed, one to which I might well aspire. My mother frequently reminded me of it: "She openeth her mouth with wisdom; and in her tongue is the law of kindness." However, if one happened to be born on one of the first seven days of any month, the verse would be very odd and inept. I had to discard this birthday idea as a mere tradition—an interesting one, nevertheless! So it was that my love for this chapter began early; but I never understood it until after I was saved and filled with the Holy Spirit. Then He Himself sang this song to my heart, recreating it and interpreting it according to its original concept.

Many preachers suppose that this chapter teaches God's pattern for a "virtuous woman"—a good, industrious wife and mother. And, of course, it does. In fact, it may be interpreted and profitably applied on almost any level of understanding. However, when we have entered into a revelation and experience of the mysticism of the forty-fifth Psalm, The Song of Solomon, and Paul's and John's teachings concerning the Bride of Christ, we then realize that this chapter of Proverbs is not singing about a mere natural woman, but also about a spiritual woman. We further understand that this "woman" is not an individual, but is a choice *body of believers,* both men and women, who come into bridal union with Christ, and pass through the various ranks of that union, until they attain the highest degree of maturity and fruitfulness—that of THE QUEEN MOTHER!

"...Upon Thy right hand did stand the queen in gold of Ophir... The King's daughter is all glorious within: her clothing is of wrought gold." (Psalm 45:9,13)

Yes, the Father is preparing a beautiful, mature, adorable Queen to rule with His Son, the Lord Jesus Christ. This Queen is selected out of all nations and peoples. She is rigorously trained, tested, and prepared. (Many are called; few are chosen.) She is, as Moffatt puts it, His paragon, and she is "one." There are many "virgins" given to the King, many "concubines," a number of "queens"—all these depict varying stages or degrees of dedication to and union with the King.

"There are threescore queens, and fourscore concubines, and virgins without number. My dove, my undefiled is but one; she is the only one of her mother, she is the choice one of her that bare her. The daughters saw her, and blessed her; yea, the queens and the concubines, and they praised her." (Song of Solomon 6:8,9)

This "woman," so intimately and lovingly portrayed, is to be chosen as the consort of the King of Kings. She is to stand at His right hand, sharing His kingdom and glory. There were those among Jesus' disciples who contended about who should be worthy of the coveted place at His right hand. He, wisely, did not answer them directly, but made it clear that this honor was at the disposition of the Father alone. Psalm forty-five reveals that this place is reserved for The Queen Mother, and that her favor and glory and reward are great.

On Her Coronation Day it will be surprising to discover that in this select company are some of the lowliest and most obscure of saints—hidden ones who were unknown and unsung among men, but well known to heaven and the King! Everyone will then be able to see that the King's favor is upon them, that He greatly desires their beauty—a beauty which is a reflection and projection of His own loveliness and grace. It is this elect Body who will bear His full name, and it is She who, in union with Christ, will make her sons princes in the earth. It is She who, with Him, will be honored and blessed by all generations. (Psalm 45:16,17)

The portrait of this Elect Lady is worthy of close study; no mere cursory glance at it will satisfy us, once we have caught a glimpse of her favor and glory. So, with hushed hearts we listen to the golden words once uttered by a queen mother to a royal beloved son of her prayers and vows. She is utterly devoted to him and deeply concerned that he find a bride worthy to become his complement, his consort, and the mother of his princely sons. She begins her theme with sound instruction regarding his own personal responsibility and integrity. Then she paints a picture of the woman he is to choose to share his heart and his throne. With the skill of a great master she creates this portrait of his bride—a woman of virtue, fidelity, industry, ability, beauty, wisdom, imagination, strength, skill and kindness. It recalls to my mind a few of Wordsworth's lines:

> "A perfect woman, nobly planned,
> To warn, to comfort, and command;

And yet a spirit still, and bright
With something of angelic light."

This noble and desirable creature is not a mere ornament of vanity; but a vessel unto honor, fit to grace the house of a king. The queen-mother does not stress the youthful charms and allurements of a blushing bride, for she knows that such attributes quickly fade; instead, she emphasizes the qualities that make up perfect wifehood and motherhood. If we apply this description to the Bride of Christ, we readily agree that She is not a delightful child; nor is She a glamor-girl, nor a career-girl—types frequently found among modern women. Among the Lord's people we encounter some who seem to want to dwell in a state of perpetual delight in the Lord's love for themselves. They desire a spiritual experience which corresponds with that of courtship in the natural realm. Such souls enjoy the beautiful, rapturous, joyous delights that are shared by those who behold Christ as Bridegroom, and betroth themselves unto Him, in expectation of complete union with Him. But, like the Shulamite in the Song of Solomon, they are slow to open the door of their heart when, in reality, He draws near. They shun the inevitable responsibilities, labors, burdens and sufferings that attend actual wifehood and motherhood.

Those of us who have become mothers, in the natural realm, know that our days of courtship and honeymoon passed swiftly and differed considerably from the later years of our married life. We learned that in order to establish a home and raise a family we were required to relinquish many of the joys and privileges we knew as a bride. It is much the same in the spiritual realm. Union with Christ does begin with much surprise, delight, ecstasy and wonderment. The tryst in the "garden" is so individual, so secret, so rapturous, that it can never be entirely shared with another soul.

"He walks with me and He talks with me,
And He tells me I am His own;
And the joys we share as we tarry there
No one other has ever known."

However, as our life of union with Christ progresses, there is ever increasing responsibility. The more intimately we come to know our Heavenly Husband, the more we participate in His sufferings, as is the case with any devoted wife. Bringing forth His sons and daughters, establishing His royal House, entering into His work and warfare, involves the loss of many of the thrilling delights of the early courtship. Yet there is a great compensation for the faithful "wife" of the Lord—a closer love, a deeper understanding, a participating with Him in His travail, a sharing of His own pain and glory.

There are many who are *known of Him,* but few who really *know Him.* Paul cried out, "... that I may know Him!" Only the saints who enter into this realm are qualified to bring forth His royal sons and daughters. And it is they who shall "take the Kingdom and possess it forevermore." To have the *revelation* of these truths is not enough; there must be an *experiential knowledge* of them, wrought within our *very being*—an actual entering into union and divine fruition here on earth, prior to the outward setting up of His Kingdom. In every age there were a few who qualified for this calling. Often they were unknown by their own generation, as was the little queen-mother of the House of David who brought forth "great David's greater Son." Yet all succeeding generations have called her blessed. So shall it be with those who, out of all ages, compose the Body of Zion's Queen.

Behold! The portrait is about to be unveiled. We silence our own thoughts and focus our attention on this Masterpiece of divine art. Slowly the curtain is drawn back, and for a few moments we are dazzled by the glory of the portrait. Then, as our eyes gradually accustom themselves to the halo of light around her, we begin to scrutinize the details of this picture. Oh, may our consideration of it be that of the connoisseur rather than that of the tyro! We observe that the first stroke of the brush was one of bold outline—a woman of virtue! The Hebrew version of the text indicates strength, firmness and ability. We realize that this is a composite woman—and in her we catch a glimpse of lovely Ruth, and recall the memorable words spoken to her:

"And now, my daughter, fear not; I will do to thee all that thou requirest; for all the city of my people doth know that thou art a virtuous woman." (Ruth 3:11)

We remember that Ruth's virtue was wrought out in suffering, deprivation and fidelity to her spiritual mother, Naomi-Mara, and in the forsaking of her own people and land and ways. Furthermore, she was absolutely obedient to the instructions of her "mother," and she abandoned her own will and reasoning, even to the point of seeming indiscretion and danger. Yet, in all this, her faith, purity, and humility were in no wise marred. Her reward? A rich one! She became the mother of Obed, who later became the grandfather of David. Thus Ruth attained a place in the House of David. She became an ancestress of Jesus Christ!

A virtuous woman! Such a one is valued far above rubies or any of the precious jewels which adorn the King's crown. *"The heart of her husband doth safely trust in her, so that he shall have no need of spoil."* To His queen-bride our Lord entrusts His sacred heart; to her He reveals His most hidden mysteries, secrets and desires. He has no fear that she will betray Him, nor bring loss to Him. She is discreet, modest, quiet—a woman of few words. Like Mary, she ponders "these things" in her heart, and does not foolishly publish them abroad. Many well-meaning souls have been disqualified for close union with the King because they did not keep His secrets. "The secret of the Lord is with them that fear Him."

Furthermore, His queen will do Him good and not evil all the days of her life. In the Moffatt version we read, "She will bring Him profit and no loss all the days of her life." Her devotion and obedience is not capricious and spasmodic; but is steadfast, consistent, enduring. As we examine ourselves in the white light of Truth, most of us realize how unprofitable and faulty we have been, and that we have brought much sorrow, loss and hindrance to our Beloved Lord—yes, even when our intention was to do Him good. We are pained to see that our neglect has affected His household, His precious children, and His Kingdom enterprizes. Yes, we readily admit that we have been more of a liability than an asset to Him, at least at times. We repent of our failures with godly sorrow, and seek an experience of consecration unto Him wherein we shall not repeat our past failures. Then, and only then, do we begin to qualify for this High Calling of God. So long as we are confident of ourselves, and assume that we are well-pleasing to God, we are in danger of deception. One of the greatest delusions that has fallen upon the present-day saints of God is the Laodicean conceit:

"Because thou sayest, I am rich and increased with goods, and have need of nothing; and knowest not that thou art wretched, and miserable, and poor, and blind, and naked: I counsel thee to buy of me gold tried in the fire (the wrought gold in which the queen is robed), that thou mayest be rich: and white raiment (the white linen of inwrought, as well as imputed, righteousness), and that the shame of thy nakedness do not appear, and anoint thine eyes with eye salve, that thou mayest see." (Revelation 3:17,18)

The higher the calling, the higher its qualifications. Those who are novices in the realm of the Spirit are often overconfident of their gifts and attainments. But the more one grows up into Christ and grasps the meaning of the Scriptures, the more humble and self-searching one becomes. The apostle Paul was favored and gifted and honored above all who lived in his day. Yet with what meekness, what restraint he spoke of himself! He did not count himself to have attained, but ran the race to the end, realizing, as perhaps no other man could, what it meant to attain "the *high* calling of God in Christ Jesus."

If we have been apprehended of Christ and have been summoned to become a part of the Throne Company, then we will be among the most humble and lowly of His followers. The Queen of God does not rely on visions, anointings, revelations and experiences of His power and blessing. She knows that the Kingdom of Heaven is on a realistic basis. His Word, sharp, quick and powerful, has cut through her complacency again and again, revealing the inner motives of her heart. She knows that the Father will be satisfied with nothing short of the *nature* of His Son, wrought in her very being. She knows also that He is a prudent husbandman and that He requires of her an abundance of *good fruit.* Yes, she is a "ten-talent servant," and she will receive a hundred-fold reward. But she will never presume to glory in her reward. She will lay it all at the feet of her Lord, knowing that it is rightfully His.

We take another close look at Her portrait: "She seeketh wool and flax and worketh willingly with her hands." Although she is a queen, she is also a worker. No idle hours for her! She sets the example for all her admiring household. Jesus said, "My Father worketh hitherto, and I work." His Bride is activated by the same divine urge. However, she does not labor in the unprofitable energy of the flesh, nor according to the ways of man—but in the power of the Holy Spirit. She is always aware that it is God that worketh in her, for she ceases from her own vain works and thoughts and ways.

She enters into "the Rest (Sabbath) prepared for the people of God." But this does not mean that she remains empty and idle. When the Spirit is not active within her, she remains in a quiet, worshipful attitude toward Him, waiting for His moving. At His slightest stir she yields herself to Him, cooperating fully with His desires. Thus, she never becomes restless during the seemingly empty and barren times which all souls experience. Nor does she clutter up her mind and her time with all sorts of activities, interests and hobbies of her own devising. She is always at the Spirit's beck and call. No task is too common, nor too exalted for her. And everything God does in and through her is a "work of faith, a labor of love."

"She is like the merchant's ships, bringing her food from afar." Yes, she does indeed bring her food from afar! She feeds her household upon "the hidden manna," the Living Word of God, which comes down out of heaven. And she drinks from the crystal fountain that flows from the high mount of God. She cannot tolerate the spoiled food, the "poison in the pot," cooked up by the would-be prophets; nor does she ever partake of the fouled water offered to the flock by the false shepherds. (No offense is intended toward the true prophets and shepherds of the Lord.)

"She riseth also while it is yet night, and giveth meat to her household, and a portion to her maidens." She knows the power of watching with God during the night seasons, and of rising to seek Him early in the morning. She is up with the dawn, preparing the meat for her family. They never lack their "meat in due season," if they will receive it from her loving hands. And her household is able to assimilate the meat, as well as the milk, of the Word. They wax strong and render valiant service to the King. They are aroused, ready, armed for the New Day of His power!

"She considereth a field and buyeth it." This woman knows the way of prayer-conquest. "The field is the world," Jesus declared. But, sad to say, it is largely in the hands of the enemy! It must be bought back, redeemed, with the gold of purified faith. The Queen knows that her Lord has said, "Ask of me, and I will give thee the nations for thine inheritance, and the uttermost parts of the earth for thy possession." So she asks and purchases her own portion of this field. Likewise, "With the fruit of her hands she planteth a vineyard." She is an expert planter. And it is The True Vine that she plants. She delights in preparing her vineyard for her Beloved. She shall not lack for new wine to offer as a sacrifice to the Lord, or to give to her household to drink.

"She girdeth her loins with strength, she strengtheneth her arms." Such words call to mind visions of Deborah, Jael, Judith, Joan of Arc, and other women who in times of crisis became valiant in warfare. They, who in their time, typified this regnant woman, "were strong in the Lord and in the power of His might." There is no faltering in the Queen, no fainting. She, even when weak, says, "I am strong in the Lord," and rises to the occasion. She is able to run and to walk, or even to stand still, as God commands. She is ready for battle or for flight, as He wills. At times she is as Zion, lifting up her voice with strength. And, again, she is as Mary, keeping silent, quietly waiting for the fulfillment of the Word of the Lord.

"She perceiveth that her merchandise is good; her candle goeth not out by night." The Moffatt version reads: "The candle burns all night in her house." Praise God! Her very life is a candle of the Lord, set upon a stand, giving light to all who are in His house. It is written that the House of David shall never lack a light! The Queen's candle shines out bravely into the world's darkness—a beacon light leading many weary, wandering ones safely home.

"She layeth her hands to the spindle and her hands hold the distaff... She is not afraid of the snow for her household; for all her household are clothed with scarlet." It is her delight to clothe her royal family in a befitting manner. The precious garments of the Spirit are painstakingly spun and woven. No ready-made, man-designed religious garments for her household! Much labor and skill are required for their fashioning. When the cold winter months come she has no fear, for all her family are provided with bright warm woolen garments. (Double garments, according to Revised Version.)

However, in spite of her labors for the royal family, she does not neglect those who are not so close to the King. "She stretcheth out her hand to the poor; yea, she reacheth forth her hands to the needy." She is ever mindful of the needs of the hungry and poor-in-spirit. Her charity abounds more and more as she is blessed and increased by God. She shelters the orphans and strangers when they find their way, as did Ruth, into the King's household.

Meanwhile, although this generous Lady labors like a servant, she is clad like a queen. She is never careless about her own attire. "Let your garments be always white; and let your head lack no oil." She wears the white linen of righteousness and "maketh herself coverings of tapestry; her clothing is silk and purple." In the days of Solomon only the nobility could afford to wear purple, due to the high cost of the dye. Even in our own day royal purple is still the principal coronation color. Frequently the Lord's queen dons her beautiful garments of praise. She adorns herself with ornaments of grace and makes herself beautiful for the eyes of the King. "So shall the King greatly desire her beauty."

"Her husband is known in the gates, when he sitteth among the elders of the land." Indeed! For He is none other than Jesus Christ, whose glory and honor is to be celebrated throughout the entire universe—the King of Kings! Yet, at this present time, He is often dishonored and disregarded upon earth. So His Queen sees to it that His Name is acclaimed and honored in every place where she sets foot. And she conducts herself in such a way as to be a credit and glory unto Him. When she is honored and praised she promptly attributes it all to her Husband.

"Strength and honor are her clothing; and she shall rejoice in time to come." I like an old translation (Jewish) which renders this verse, "She shall laugh at the last days." Moffatt says, "Strong and secure is her position; looking ahead, she can afford to laugh." Yes, "The Highest Himself shall establish her." This is where Sarah, "the mother from above," comes into the picture. Once, it is true, she laughed in unbelief. But, after her faith was purified, there came a day when she laughed and rejoiced with holy joy. Her Isaac (laughter) was born to her and God's promise was fulfilled. The Queen is strong in rejoicing. Frequently the Spirit moves her to holy laughter. And often when things seem to be the darkest and most oppressive, her joyful shouts and lilting songs can be heard. Because she knows how to "rejoice in hope," she can also be "patient in tribulation, continuing instant in prayer." Her strength arises out of the joy of the Lord. And she, God's Zion, can well afford to praise God and to "smile at all her foes."

"She openeth her mouth with wisdom, and in her tongue is the law of kindness." How eloquent are these words! This phrase seems to parallel that of Psalm forty-five which says of the King, "Grace is poured into His lips." James has declared that if a man offends not with his tongue, the same is a perfect man, able to bridle his entire body. "How forcible are right words!" How creative! How healing! How uplifting! Yet, what a world of trouble and mischief lies within the domain of the tongue! It can be a fountain of life, or a poisoned stream of death. It can be a fruitful tree, or a venomous shrub.

Those who grow up into Christ learn to glorify Him in both words and deeds. They learn to set a watch by the door of their lips. They do not indulge in idle, foolish, or harmful conversation. Their words become fewer as they become wiser. The Queen is not a gushy woman. She never uses her tongue to pierce or lash others. Her words are words of life, words of wisdom, spoken out of the abundance of her heart's treasure. And in her words, as in the Word of the King, there is power. The first Eve spoke enticing words to her spouse, and thus deprived her children of the right to eat of the "Tree of Life." But the second Eve, Bride of the Second

Adam, shall speak unto her children the words of eternal life, and lead them into Paradise, where they may eternally partake of the wondrous Tree.

"She looketh well to the ways of her household, and eateth not the bread of idleness." She sees to it that the members of her family are diligent, alert and well ordered. At this very hour she is being used to set the King's House in order in preparation for His approaching visitation and appearing!

"Her children rise up and call her blessed; her husband also, and he praiseth her." Mother Zion shall soon be revealed in open glory. Her children will come from the ends of the earth and gather to honor and bless her. It was the custom in Israel to hold the mother of the family in high esteem, and for her children to obey and pay tribute to her. This custom was carried over into Christianity and has reached its highest practice among the nations that honor Christ. The natural is but a type of the spiritual. Next to the King, Queen Mother Zion is to receive the highest honor and glory in the Kingdom of Heaven. The saints who attain to the high calling of this company will actually partake of the eternal glory of Christ, being made co-heirs, co-rulers, co-creators with Him. Their spiritual children shall be the first to praise them. Their divine Husband Himself shall praise them in this manner: "Many daughters have done virtuously, but thou excellest them all."

Natural talents and abilities play no part in the choice of this Queen. By grace alone can one qualify for this high calling of God. Many may aspire to it, but none shall attain it except by the will of God and complete consecration to Him. This Queen leaves all for Him: her father's house, her former family, her own ways and desires. "He is thy Lord; and worship thou Him." The one consuming motive of her heart is that of worship. She is a Mary who chooses "the better part which can never be taken away;" she is an Abigail who hastens forth to serve the King and to bring Him her best fruits and wines; a Rebecca who is willing to go into a far land and forget her dearest earthly ties. These women, to some measure at least, followed the Bible "blueprint" drawn by the Master. For, of course, He is the original Artist who created the Queen's Portrait. And all who fit into the picture shall be designed for that place by the same Master hand.

No one ever fitted the picture more perfectly and completely than the little Queen of the House of David. Her humility, purity, simplicity, and complete consecration unto God have set the example for all who follow in the Queen's train. Her children have arisen in every generation to call her blessed. And her husband has caused her to be praised wherever His Word has been revealed. By carefully studying the picture drawn of her in Luke's gospel we can come to an understanding of what the Father desires of each of us. He did not choose Mary casually nor by mere chance; nor was Gabriel's salutation only a compliment. In the original text we find that his words indicate that she was much graced and acceptable unto God. The requirements of the Kingdom are exacting, and the qualifications for the Queen, even more so. A provision has been made whereby we also, through Jesus Christ, may be full of grace and highly favored of God. But it is only by yielding ourselves unto Him as she did, and living our entire life in the light of such a consecration, that we can be found acceptable. Her fiat echoes within our own being as we repeat the memorable words, "Behold the handmaiden of the Lord; be it unto me according to Thy Word."

We have beheld the Queen's portrait. We have examined it; pondered over it; marvelled at its esquisite beauty; reveled in its splendor. She is all-glorious within and without. But, after all, we have seen only a picture, a likeness. What a consummate joy will be ours on her Coronation Day. Then "With gladness and rejoicing shall they be brought; they shall enter into the King's palace." We too hope to be in that elect number. Then shall all the nations rejoice to behold Zion's King and Queen, ruling both in heaven and earth with equity and love. And then shall the closing words of our song be fulfilled: "Give her the fruit of her hands, and let her own works praise her in the gates."

QUEEN-BRIDE

"Come hither, and I will show thee the bride, the Lamb's wife." (Revelation 21:9)

> Behold the bride of the Lamb—
> The pride of the Great I Am!
> Let heaven sing forth the praise
> And magnify the grace
> Of the High and Holy One
> Who formed her for His Son.
>
> Behold this Virgin of Light
> In garments of glistening white!
> And hail her nuptial day,
> When the Bridegroom shall catch her away
> To make her His holy bride
> And enthrone her at His side.
>
> Behold her scepter and crown,
> Her favor and her renown!
> By prophets long foretold
> She, clothed in Ophir's gold,
> As Zion's queen shall stand
> Upon the King's right hand.

Behold this mother of sons
The chosen, anointed ones
Who are born of royal birth
And shall reign as kings in the earth.
Come, adore her with holy love,
This queen-bride mother from above.

—F.M.

THE ADORNED BRIDE

FRANCES METCALFE

"Come hither, and I will show thee the bride, the Lamb's wife... Prepared as a bride, adorned for her husband."

WHO IS SHE?

Who is she, my lovely bride,
Hidden away in the earth?
Where is she, my joy and pride,
My jewel of matchless worth?
Graceful, pure, and beautiful is she,
Robed in garments of white,
Like a brilliant star shining from afar
With clear and radiant light.
Blessed, thrice blessed is she,
My queen, My holy bride;
Blessed, thrice blessed is she,
Soon to appear at My side.

Who is she, fair as the moon,
Shining through earth's darkest night?
Whence comes she, arising soon,
Clothed with the Sun's glory-light?
She is My bride, My pearl, My only one.
Bought with My own precious blood,
Ever to abide at My riven side,
Eternal queen of God.
Blessed, thrice blessed is she,
My queen, My holy bride;
Blessed, thrice blessed is she,
Soon to appear at My side.

INTRODUCTION

The mystical bride of Christ as revealed in the Pauline epistles, the Song of Solomon, and the 45th Psalm, is obviously a composite body of elect souls who are called, chosen and faithful. The Holy Spirit uses the sacrament of marriage—with all that it entails of wooing, courtship, betrothal and consummation—as the beautiful symbol of the love of Adonai, the Bridegroom-God, for each elect soul. In the Old Testament this love-life of God is directed toward Zion. In the New Testament the bride of Christ becomes the elect lady of the heart of God.

The Holy Spirit personalizes the truths of Scripture to the individual members of the Bride Company. In manifold and mysterious ways every redeemed soul is led through servitude into discipleship; from discipleship into friendship; from friendship into sonship; from sonship into the bridal state of complete union with God. In the light of this truth, all souls are seen to be feminine toward God as they are mated with Him—they being the negative-passive; He being the eternal positive-active. In the realm of nature it has been observed that the moon is purely feminine in relationship to the sun, but masculine in relationship to the earth, influencing seasons and tides. Likewise, the Bride is often referred to as the spiritual moon who reflects the light of the Sun of Righteousness to the world.

The call, "Behold the Bridegroom cometh, go ye out to meet Him!" has echoed and reechoed in the hearts of the saints throughout the centuries, but at no time has it resounded so insistently as it has during the past few years. Waiting hearts everywhere believe that soon another call will sound with trumpet blast, "The marriage of the Lamb has come!" Blessed are they who shall be found prepared and ready to go in with Him before the door is shut.

BRING ME A BRIDE

Bring Me a bride prepared,
Robed in garments of white;
Bring Me a maiden adorned,
Resplendent with jewels bright.
Bring Me a virgin chaste.
Pure as the falling snow:
She shall be Mine alone,
My heart's great love to know.

Bring Me a maiden fair,
Fragrant with ointments sweet;
Bring me a dove-like one,
Gentle of heart, and meek.
Crown her with precious jewels—
The rarest ones I own;
She shall be chosen queen
To share My royal throne.

"I decked thee also with ornaments, and I put bracelets upon thy hands, and a chain on thy neck. And I put a jewel on thy forehead, and earrings in thine ears, and a beautiful crown upon thine head. Thus wast thou decked with gold and silver; and thy raiment was of fine linen, and silk, and broidered work; thou didst eat fine flour, and honey, and oil: and thou wast exceeding beautiful, and thou didst prosper into a kingdom. And thy renown went forth among the heathen for thy beauty: for it was perfect through My comeliness, which I had put upon thee, saith the Lord God." (Ezekiel 16: 11-14)

THE ADORNED BRIDE

"Can a maid forget her ornaments, or a bride her attire." (Jer. 2:32)

The resplendent attire of the queen-bride is vividly portrayed in the 45th Psalm: "The King's daughter is all glorious within: her clothing is of wrought gold. She shall be brought unto the King in raiment of needlework." And in The Revelation we read: "The marriage of the Lamb is come, and His wife hath made herself ready. And to her was granted that she should be arrayed in fine linen, clean and white." In addition to her beautiful garments the bride is to be adorned with precious jewels—the ornaments of grace which will enhance her beauty in the eyes of the King. As Eliezer adorned Rebekah for Isaac, and as the Eunuch adorned Esther for Ahasuerus, so the Holy Spirit adorns those who are called as His bride. An ornament is defined as: "That which is added to embellish or beautify; to decorate and enhance." The queen-bride, desirous to win the love and favor of the King and to give Him pleasure, is now in her chamber hidden away from the eyes of the world. A few close attendants are assisting her in her final preparation. Blessed is the bride who shall be found bathed, anointed, robed, and ornamented, ready for the holy nuptials.

HUMILITY

Among the ornaments of grace which are becoming to the choice bride, none is more costly than *humility*; none more gratifying to the King. The apostle Peter has instructed us to put on "the ornament of a meek and quiet spirit which is of *great price* in the sight of the Lord." This meekness is a humility of heart and mind and will, and is a rare grace among even mature saints. It does not concern itself with outward acts of apparent meekness: but is a constant attitude of heart and mind, unconsciously manifest in every thought and act and word. Few in the earth are lavishly ornamented with this virtue. The higher the calling, the more difficult it is to walk humbly. The greater the spiritual attainments and gifts, the greater is the temptation to become high-minded and exalted in thought. Humility is an ornament which can never be fashioned by self-effort. It must be a genuine work of the Holy Spirit, inwrought by painful and persistent operation. For this cause was the apostle Paul given a thorn in the flesh. So great were his attainments and revelations that, in spite of his constant desire to remain the "least of the saints" (although in reality he was the greatest of the apostles), the Father deemed it necessary to give him a thorn in the flesh lest he should be exalted above measure. Thorns and briars are often found in the pathway and in the flesh of the bride, and through many humiliations and vicissitudes she learns the way of meekness and humility before God and man.

As the bride advances more and more into heavenly revelations and raptures, as her calling and election is substantiated and manifest, as she is told divine mysteries and shown divine favor, she is in ever-increasing danger of becoming exalted. The beautiful grace of perfect humility is not only an ornament, but is a shield against the foe. Let her seek this humility daily, hourly. Let her walk and talk in meekness, and practice this attitude of heart continually.

In the presence of God let her abase herself utterly, being fully aware of her own complete failure and helplessness apart from His grace. Let her learn to depend upon His grace entirely. Boasting is absolutely excluded!

The true bride has a Mary-heart. She rejoices and sings her magnificat with Mary, the virgin-mother of our Lord, "He hath regarded the *low estate* of His handmaiden... He that is mighty hath done to me great things." She finds in Mary a beautiful pattern for her own relationship to God, and marks well the humility of this young maiden. When visited by the great angel and honored above all her race, favored above all other women, she cried out: "Behold the handmaid of the Lord; be it unto me according to thy word." There was no boasting, no flaunting of her favor with God—only a song of praise unto the One who abases the proud and exalts the humble. "Before honor is humility." The true bride never ceases to be amazed that she, too, has found favor with God. Her response is to place herself unreservedly in His dear hands as handmaiden, as love-slave, forever. The queen who shall stand at the King's right hand will have followed His example by emptying herself, humbling herself, becoming a servant faithful unto death. It is not so much the servant who becomes the queen, but the queen who becomes the servant, who brings joy to the heart of God. Beloved bride, above all things, fear pride and exaltation. Through these many have fallen from their high calling. Never appear before the King without the ornament of humility. How greatly shall He desire you! How beautiful you shall appear in His eyes!

UNDERSTANDING

Among the King's jewels is another beautiful heart-ornament which has been fashioned with delicate art—*understanding*. "Understanding is a wellspring of life unto him that hath it," and is of great consolation to the heart of God. Our Beloved hungers and thirsts for the love of those of an understanding heart. He desires a bride who can sympathize with Him in all His desires and purposes, sharing with Him the deepest emotions and affections of His nature. During His life here on earth there were few who offered Him such comfort. As He approached the dark hours of His passion and death, there was one among the few whose heart bled with Him; one who anointed Him aforetime for His burial; who lavished upon Him the costly fragrance from her alabaster box. So unusual was her offering, and so greatly did He appreciate it, that He caused this deed to be remembered as a lasting memorial, commanding that wherever the gospel should be preached, this act of Mary's should be proclaimed. Mary's understanding had been imparted to her during the hours in which she sat at the feet of Jesus. She, who was a pattern of the elect bride of all ages, had chosen the "better part" which could never be taken away from her. Wise, indeed, is the bride who makes the same choice today and remembers the admonition, "With all thy getting, get understanding."

Once when the Lord communed with me He spoke to me with such sadness that my own heart was deeply stirred. As nearly as I can recall, these were His words: "I long to be understood by My people, yet from the beginning they have misunderstood Me and My ways. They fear to draw near unto Me, preferring to follow Me afar off. They fear to drink fully of My love, lest it consume them. My people Israel never understood My purposes: I longed to bless them, to increase them, to favor them, to do them good; but they doubted My mercy and set aside My plans for their own. Throughout the centuries My heart has cried out for a people who could understand Me." To be misunderstood and ill-thought of is one of the most cruel sufferings that can come to a human being. Instinctively, we all search for friends who love and understand us according to the innermost desires of our hearts. Have we ever considered the sorrow we cause our Lord by our coldness and indifference and failure to properly understand Him? This ornament of grace is a mark of maturity and refinement of character. The bride-saint who walks in heart-unity, who understands His ways even when they seem strange to others, is very dear to God's heart.

GRATITUDE

No ornament becomes the bride more fittingly than that of *gratitude.* An appreciative, thankful spirit enhances the beauty of any soul. Ingratitude is most grievous to the human heart, and lack of appreciation mars every human relationship; while thankfulness and a true sense of appreciation strengthen such ties. The refined soul is an appreciative soul. A baby has no appreciation of values. All that is bestowed upon him in the way of love and affection is taken for granted. He is incapable of gratitude for his mother's pain and sacrifice; neither can he appreciate the inheritance which may be his from his father. His life is one of constant demand. This attitude continues throughout most of his childhood, and not until he has attained maturity with its suffering and responsibility does he begin to realize his indebtedness to his parents.

There is an analogy between the natural and the spiritual life. Babes in Christ have a similar incapacity to fully appreciate His great sacrificial atonement and the surpassingly great inheritance of the saints which is to be their portion. They frequently do more asking and praying than offering of thanksgiving and praise; but as they advance in the knowledge of God they should become increasingly grateful for the mercies which they enjoy. Those who come into divine union with Christ as their Bridegroom find an ever-increasing thankfulness manifest in their relationship toward Him. *The advanced bride sees nothing but the goodness of God in every circumstance.* She is fully confident that all things work together for good. She is thankful, yes, overflowing with praise regardless of the seeming adversities which befall her. Less mature souls pass lightly over gifts and blessings which would move the bride to tears of thanksgiving. How beautiful in His sight is the soul that is ornamented with this grace of overflowing thanksgiving! It is impossible that any saint could ever become too appreciative, too thankful to God for His mercy and goodness.

DISCRETION

There is another charming ornament of inestimable value which is rarely displayed, and that is *discretion*. The Word of God admonishes the bride in these words: "Discretion shall preserve thee." In the last chapter of the book of Proverbs we see the portrait of a discreet woman who "openeth her mouth with wisdom," and in whom the heart of her husband "doth safely trust." Discreet is defined as, "Possessed of or showing discernment or good judgment in conduct and especially in speech." Mary, the mother of our Lord, has left us an example of this godly virtue. She hid all these things (the secrets of God), and "pondered them in her heart." She told no one, not even Joseph her betrothed, of the angelic visitation. She subjected herself to great reproach rather than to expose the secret God had entrusted to her. She bided her time, waiting for the Lord to reveal His plan according to His own will. Contrast her caution and restraint with the glib manner in which many of the Lord's people speak of holy things. The true bride learns that "the secret of the Lord is with them that fear Him." She is disciplined and controlled by the Holy Spirit in all her actions and words which relate to the King. She does not make common the sacred things of God, and many of His favors she hides from the eyes of others. On the contrary, the immature follow their own impulses and are often unrestrained in both action and speech, thereby bringing needless confusion, and also reproach upon the Lord. Beloved bride, your wedding trousseau will never be complete without the ornament of holy discretion.

STABILITY

Stability is an ornament which can never be hidden. It is an admirable grace which commends itself alike to God and man. How comforting, encouraging and uplifting is the even, balanced walk of the stable, settled, and proved saint. The prepared bride has been exercised to such a degree that she is able to remain steadfast and unmoved in every circumstance and condition. When in the state of spiritual exaltation or transport she does not become flighty or high-minded. She is not given to elation or excessive enthusiasm. She receives divine favor and revelation quietly and reverently. She rejoices in all these things; yet is ever watchful lest, while upon the heights, she be suddenly tripped and thrown by her enemy. When undergoing tribulation, suffering, loss, or apparent desolation, she is likewise unmoved. She knows in Whom she has believed; she is settled in faith and rests confidently in God in whatever state she finds herself. In honor or dishonor, whether persecuted or highly favored, whether enriched or impoverished, she maintains her calm deliberate faith and consecration. She is equally at home in the heights or in the valley; yes, even in the wilderness she leans upon the arm of her Beloved. *She has learned to know God beyond feeling, beyond sight, beyond anointings, beyond outward manifestations.* She, this choice one, is mature, established in God—not for a season, but for eternity. Of her it may be said, "It is a joy to note your steadiness and the solid front of your faith in Christ." (Colossians 2:5, Moffatt) This blessed state commends her to the heart of the King, and great favor becomes her portion. The enemy of her soul would like to rob her of this exquisite ornament of grace. She will do well to heed the warning given by St. Peter: "Ye therefore, beloved, seeing ye know these things before, beware lest ye also, being led away with the error of the wicked, fall from your own steadfastness."

EAGERNESS

There is another lovely decoration which the Holy Spirit will bestow upon the prepared bride. We might name it the grace of *eagerness.* Our beloved Lord surpasses all others in His eagerness. He is eager to save, eager to bless, eager to baptize with His Spirit, eager to manifest Himself to us and in us, and eager to draw us unto Himself in complete union. Oh, that He had a people as eager-hearted as He! We can all picture how tried an earthly bridegroom would be if he were given a bored, listless, indifferent bride-to-be. The typical bride is blushingly happy and eager for the nuptials. She is not dubious or diffident; but glad, joyful, ready! Many find it very difficult to believe that the Lord desires to manifest His fervent love as a Bridegroom to them as individuals. They believe in the Scriptures which reveal the relationship of Christ to His bride in a general way, but cannot grasp it for themselves. They believe He has loved them enough to save them, but that He could not possibly desire the close union of lover and husband with them. The Holy Spirit continues His persistent wooing of the soul until she awakens out of her long slumber to rise and receive her divine

Lover. Having once received Him, let her not lapse into neglect and indifference. Jesus wants an eager, fervent, watchful bride. He wants her to express and demonstrate this eagerness. He wants her to anticipate the eternal joys He has prepared for her. He delights to find in her a youthful spirit of expectancy, and, if at times she must rise and run out into the night—leaving others behind in her search for Him—He is pleased and drawn the more to her because of her fervent desire.

WISDOM

The crowning ornament of the bride is *wisdom,* the tiara by which her veil is secured. "She (wisdom) shall be to thine head an ornament of grace." This crowning glory of the bride is worn upon the head in which the carnal mind, the enemy of God, has been fully subjected to the mind of Christ—the mind in which He alone reigns supreme over her entire being. Wisdom, a glorious diadem, befits the queen who is ready for the final nuptials. By wisdom the worlds were framed; by wisdom His house is built; wisdom is better than rubies, and all things that may be desired are not to be compared with it. O bride, remember that "by wisdom kings reign and decree justice." You shall not be fit to be the royal consort of the King of Kings until this crown is placed upon your head.

Comparatively few in the earth have desired and sought and obtained this gift from the Holy Spirit. The bride who obtains this prize is able to see into the hidden knowledge of God; the mysteries of the universe are open to her, and the life of the ages is her portion.

Bride-elect of the King, make sure that your trousseau is complete. Do not be found without your wedding garments. Be certain, too, that you have received from the Holy Spirit your lovely jeweled ornaments of grace. Make yourself ready for the King. Be covered with glory from head to foot, without and within—His adorned bride! Soon you shall appear before Him to ravish His heart with love. "So shall the King greatly desire thy beauty."

CHRIST AND HIS BRIDE

He is altogether lovely,
She is altogether fair;
He is chiefest of ten thousand,
And no other one with her can compare.
He loves her with complete devotion,
For she was taken from His wounded side;
And throughout eternity
They'll dwell in perfect unity—
Christ and His holy bride.

YOU

Frances Metcalfe

This little booklet, with its definitely personal title, is intended to be a definitely personal message to *you*, sent from the heart of our beloved Lord Jesus, by means of the Holy Spirit, channeled through me. It was first written four years ago, shortly before the Passover-Resurrection season. And it all began with a most unexpected "appearing" of Jesus.

I had been waiting upon Him for several days, very low at His feet indeed. For I—and those to whom I am closely joined in the Lord—had been passing through weeks, even months, of intensive testing and seeming devastation. We all were empty and barren, void of inspiration. Nevertheless we were devoting ourselves to a time of individual "retreat"—waiting on the Lord, worshiping Him. Then the Beloved suddenly drew near and spoke in a surprising way!

For many weeks the Holy Spirit continued to amplify and apply the message Jesus imparted to my heart. In a most blessed way it ministered to each of us. Now, by His leading, we are indeed glad to share it with you.

—Frances Metcalfe
Passover-Resurrection Time 1966

INTRODUCTION

Our winter, here on the mountain, had been unusually severe, and for weeks at a time we had been almost entombed with ice and snow. The winds were frequent and violent, reaching almost hurricane velocity at times. Yet the elements had not been as severe and violent as the dealings of the Spirit! What a whirlwind, what a tempest, had raged around us! And now the time of testing had passed, or at least there was a lull in the storm. There was a breath of spring in the air, and some of the bulbs were showing green shoots. As I waited on the Lord for several days, I was almost fearful of what to expect next. I knew that He had been dealing with us as *sons,* and that He faithfully chastens (child-trains) and scourges every son whom He receives. By His grace I wanted to accept and endure His correction and discipline, yes even His scourgings; but in myself I felt faint and utterly unable. So by faith I gave thanks to Him, standing on the Word that "no chastening for the present seemeth to be joyous, but grievous: nevertheless afterward it yieldeth the peaceable fruit of righteousness unto them which are exercised thereby." (Hebrews 12:11)

Then, in the midst of my giving of thanks, to my utter surprise and delight, "Jesus, Himself, drew near!" (Luke 24:15) I saw our Beloved walking in our midst—as in a garden of lilies—with great tenderness and concern. We, His lilies, were all lying in the dust, our stems broken, our blossoms trampled down.

It was as though a violent storm had beaten us and left our garden ravaged! He walked most carefully, so as not to crush even a tiny shoot. And He spoke in a whisper, as though to Himself, these words: "By reason of many breakings." Then He stooped and began to lift each stem up and brush the dust and gravel away. As He did so, He said, "I am the lifter up of your head." (Psalm 3:3)

Although He spoke no other words, He conveyed His thoughts to me by the Spirit. I shall try to relate them, though no words can possibly give them the color and meaning they had to my illumined heart. He reminded me that the epitome of all knowledge and wisdom is to KNOW GOD—Who and What He is and was and ever shall be. "That I may *know* Him!" cried our father St. Paul, and every saint reechoes that cry. This is the first and great essential. And a second, like unto it is, "Know *thyself!*" The basic cry in the heart of man in every generation is, "Who am I, what am I, whither have I come, and where am I going?"

Our knowledge of God has steadily increased, as the Holy Spirit has graciously taught us, year after year. Many have been His appearings, movings and revelations. He has unveiled to us His Sacred Name, in its compound meanings, and His essential self-existence and glory. At times we have been almost overwhelmed with His holiness, wisdom and power. Especially had He been manifest in our midst during the preceding autumn, when, for a period of several weeks, the Spirit unveiled Him to us in great glory. As is always the case when we draw near to God, we were *reduced* as He was *magnified.* He increased! We decreased! Our self-nature became increasingly desolate and abhorrent in our eyes. We were blasted by the heat of His fiery sun. We were prostrated by the downpour of His mighty rain, His hail, and the increasing weight of His snow, which turned to ice and entombed us!

Now, suddenly, in resurrection life and love, our Lord appeared, in the midst of our garden, to lift us up, prop us up by His love, and prepare us for a time of beautiful blossoming and fragrance. All praise to His glorious Name!

This visitation of the Lord was so real, so vivid to my inner eyes, that I remained for several hours in meditation. The Spirit brought before me each one of our Candlestick fellowship, and in a most tender way He manifested His loving concern to lift up their heads and their hearts. Then His love flowed on out through my heart and mind, to all the members of His precious Body who were undergoing crushing experiences, who were cast down, bruised or broken. The next day He inspired me to write my impressions. And for days this writing, this special message, continued to develop.

Jesus knows exactly how worthless, useless and barren we sometimes feel! How unimportant! How profitless as a servant! How barren as a wife! How immature as a son! He knows that in the obscurity and humiliation of this, our hidden calling, we may easily lose our identity and our personal sense of destiny. Oh yes, we know *His* worth! Oh yes, we fully believe in and accept the teaching of the Word and the Spirit about the worth of His Church, His Bride, His Sons. But more and more we tend to separate this awareness from ourselves as an individual, and to lose the vital sense of our *individual* value to Him. We learn painfully, day by day, to know our old nature with its utterly contemptible weaknesses and failures. This, it is true, is the negative side of self-knowledge. But, praise God, there is a positive side also. In Christ Jesus we are amazing *new creations,* and, as such, our worth, our desirability, our beauty, in His eyes, is beyond all the telling. However, Jesus Himself has risen up to attempt to tell us in His own precious ways!

Do not apply what He says to certain ones who seem especially spiritual to you—but directly to *yourself.* I can't stress this point too much, for Jesus wants you to receive these things very personally and intimately, as directly from Himself to *you.* It is false and hypocritical humility that causes us to belittle ourselves unduly. It is good that we have had our spiritual and natural pride broken again and again. Better to stay forever in the dust than to arise again to any form of self-pride! But, surely, there is *grace* in Christ to enable us to rise up and accept and receive all that He has provided for us personally—as well as collectively—in the *new creation*. And, at this time He desires that we do just this. After reading, meditating, and praying about each little "capsule" of wisdom, do wait upon Him and seek the confirmation and further illumination of the Holy Spirit.

YOU ARE HIS CHOSEN ONE

You, individually, personally, have been *chosen* by YHVH Himself. "Ye have not chosen Me, but I have chosen you, and ordained you." Just as Jesus spoke these words to each of His Apostles—in spite of their doubts, sins, faults and failings—so He speaks these words to *you*. You have not found Him; He has found you, and not by accident! The Creator and Sustainer of the entire universe painstakingly sought for you and drew you unto Himself. Out of all earth's benighted millions of souls, He chose you! Say it with awe, "I am His favored, His chosen one!" Say it with joy! Say it with faith! And every day lift up your heart and head in the awareness of His incredible *personal love* and *desire* for you—as though there were no other. As one writer put it: "Think of it; you, with all your lusts, angers, envies, jealousies, and sloth; you with all your meanness, pettiness, towering pride; you with all your covetousness; you who can be at times a glutton; you with all your secret ambitions for earthly approval and glory, your sly schemings, your craving for worldly wealth and ease; you who so reek of the earth—you are surpassingly and uniquely dear and desirable unto Him." You are His chosen one!

Many times we feel as cheap as the chemicals that make up our aging bodies. Some witty scientist figured out that our body is composed of lime enough to make six bars of soap; iron enough to fashion a half-dozen ten-penny nails; phosphorous enough for twenty boxes of matches; sugar enough to sweeten ten cups of coffee; just enough potassium to explode a toy cannon; and sufficient sulphur to deflea one fair-sized dog. The price of these chemicals would be about 87 cents! We have laughed about this and felt it was a pretty fair estimate—though someone who loved us might say that we were worth a million to them! However, only recently, scientists have become more enlightened. The atomic age is unlocking amazing secrets. While it is true that these chemicals in their present state are worth only this amount, their *potential* value—the unlocking of *the atomic power stored in them*—is more than *one billion dollars!* We can't even grasp what this amount of money means, let alone appreciate the fact that *the Lord has given each one of us a billion dollar physical body.*

If this is the value of the body, what is the value of the soul and of the New Creation which is clothed by this physical structure? When I first read this scientific statement, I immediately lifted up my soul in high praise to our marvelous God. And now the Spirit has reminded me of it, so that I may relate it to you. Quit going around feeling like 87 cents! Awake to the awareness that God has invested more than a billion dollars in your body alone. It is said that the processes which are being carried on at any given moment *in one single nerve cell* of your body are more complicated and involved than all the complex processes of all the complex machines and electronic devices man has ever invented! Try to grasp this. You are fearfully and wonderfully made!

You are a living, breathing, walking, talking WONDER! Don't grovel like a worm, but lift up your heart and your head and give awed praise unto the Creator, as never before!

YOU ARE A BRANCH IN THE LIVING VINE

On the eve of His Passion, in His last love-weighted words, Jesus said to His chosen ones, "I am the Vine, you are the branches." And to *you* He says it just as certainly, "You are a branch of Me." At first thought, it may seem of little importance to be compared to a trailing branch of a grapevine, destined to be strictly pruned, cut back and disciplined to entwine around a cross-shaped stick, bent low with a load of dusty grapes. But when we consider that Jesus said, "I am the Vine," then this becomes vastly significant. He is the Living Vine Who shall fill the face of the earth with fruit. He himself was called in the Old Testament, "My Servant, the Branch." And now He calls you too, "My servant, a branch." He has shared this glorious prophetic name with you! Furthermore, you didn't just naturally grow in this Heavenly Vine—you had to be cut and grafted in by the skillful, painstaking hand of the Husbandman, God the FATHER—the great Eternal One! He cut you off from a wild vine and grafted you into His Son! Between the branch and the Vine there exists *the most intimate and personal relationship possible.* His life is constantly, each hour and moment, flowing into you and through you. Otherwise you would wilt and die and be cut off and destroyed.

Because you are a branch in the True Vine, there is no possible way that you can keep from bearing fruit! (Unless, of course, you deliberately refuse to abide in Him.) Isn't it time to stop feeling bedraggled and grieved about your fruitless state? The Lord has been reducing all of us to a place of utter barrenness and loss within ourselves. But, praise God, in Christ He has ordained that you shall not only bear *some* fruit but *much* fruit, and that "your fruit may abide." You can't see it? You can't feel it? Well, neither can a grape vine. It just feels the cut of the pruning knife and, later, the dust and heaviness, the bowing down. The Husbandman is seeking for the precious fruits of the Spirit, and these are not discernible to the natural man. "You are My branch," He says, therefore rejoice in your *certain fruitfulness* and quit feeling barren and useless. There is an old song that says, "Only a branch, I'm only a branch, only a branch in the Living Vine; Love flowing free from His heart to mine—I'm only a branch in the Vine." Only!

YOU ARE GOD'S FIELD

The Beloved Apostle Paul had a lot to say about "YOU." And this ought not to surprise you, for the Holy Spirit has always applied His words to Christians in every age. "You," says St. Paul, "are God's field (or garden) to be planted." (1 Cor. 3:9) "You are God's garden and vineyard and field under cultivation." (Amplified) He is the Husbandman—a term He seems to delight to use. He is the farmer who is intimately associated with "the good earth" from which He formed man. In a larger sense, the whole world is His field. But most of it has grown wild because of the sowing of Satan. It has produced a harvest of evil. Field by field the Husbandman, our "Goel," redeems each little plot of ground and carefully cultivates it. You are a little miniature world, an individual field, redeemed by His precious blood at great cost. You are His "eretz ahdam" (red earth), His "terra sancta" (holy land.) You are *doubly dear* to Him since He both *created* you and *redeemed* you. "God so loved the world (the field)... " God *so* loves *you*, His world and field. Think how painstakingly He has cultivated you, breaking up the fallow ground again and again, taking out the rocks and sticks, plowing deeply. Like the Psalmist, you have felt the furrows deep in your heart, you have seen the fruit of your own planting plowed under and left to decay. The Husbandman knows that your soil will be barren, unless it is well *fertilized*. And for His soil-conditioning He uses no synthetic chemicals, but the *organic richness of decaying matter.* You had hoped to be rid of the things to which you had to die. But no! They have been withered and plowed under to decay within. And you at times have felt the stench, the loathsomeness of this prolonged death.

But all this was done in wisdom and love, to prepare you for the planting of the most precious and choice Seed ever provided by God! In your field, as in the virgin soil of Mary, the Husbandman is sowing the very Seed of Christ. In Mary only one Seed was sown. But now that He has been raised, and the Seed has been multiplied, the Father sows Him again and again in His prepared fields. Think of it! Growing in you right now is this choice grain of wheat—Christ Jesus! And His rising is not to be in a *single* form, but *multiplied* even in *you!* Did not our Lord say that He was the Sower? The seed He sows will bring forth fruit, for the Father is the Husbandman and will cultivate the soil, plant the seed and send the needed rain of the Spirit. Praise God! However, in some fields the fruit will be only forty-fold, in some sixty-fold, and in some a hundred-fold. If, in spite of all the cultivation, hard, stony soil remains in your heart—by reason of your own resistance, stubbornness or hardening—and if you fall easily under temptations, your fruit will be scant. If the love of the things and pleasures of the world, or if concern over the cares of life crowd out the precious seed, the harvest cannot be full. However, praise God, the Spirit strongly witnesses that Jesus desires you to be a field of "good ground... which in an honest and good heart, having heard the word, keep it, and bring forth fruit with patience." (Luke 8:15) Yes, even a hundred-fold!

YOU ARE AN EPISTLE OF CHRIST

When Paul told the Corinthians that they were "the epistle of Christ... written not with ink, but with the Spirit of the living God" (2 Cor. 3:3), he stated a profound truth that few of us have fully grasped. You too are a living epistle that can be "known and read of all men!" No doubt you, as we, have found that the Holy Spirit has faithfully led you not only to read, but also to *eat,* the written Word of the Lord. He has quickened the Word and made it Spirit and Life. The Logos, the Living Word, is Christ Jesus, with whom you, and we, are united. And at times surely you have sensed, as we have, that your heart and mind have been made tablets on which the Spirit is writing the sacred Scriptures in this age.

The New Covenant is thus written in men. (Hebrews 8:8-10) And not only is the Covenant written upon our minds and hearts but, also, in a wondrous way, *all Scripture* is gradually engraved within our being. All that the historians have recorded and the prophets have spoken, in the Old Testament, finds some form of expression in us; all the words of Jesus, the teachings of the Apostles, yes, even the Revelation of John—bit by bit, line by line, is imparted unto us. Oh may the Word become flesh in us indeed!

One time the Spirit came upon me in a most unusual way and instructed me to say (in union with my Lord), "Lo I, Frances, come. In the volume of *the Book* it is written of *me.*" (Psalm 40:7) It is true! In the volume of God's Book it is written of *you.* Before the world's foundation you were known and loved and chosen in Christ. You too are becoming a living Word, a living Epistle, of Christ. It is true that you are not yet known and read of all men. But most certainly you are known and read of saints and angels.

At another time, the Spirit said to me, "Seek ye out the book of the Lord, and read." (Isaiah 34:16) Since I was spending much time studying the Bible, I did not understand this command at first. But it brought me into a blessed revelation. Instead of turning me to the written Word, the Spirit at that time turned me to His living epistles. He taught me to regard each member of Christ's Body as a page, a portion of His great Book. I began to learn how to decipher and read, in part at least, that which He is writing in each chosen one. It was a breath-taking experience! And in myself I kept crying out, "Oh, to be read aright!" For, of course, I realized more fully than before that I too was an epistle, a little book within *The Book*. There is a modern saying, "Do you read me?" What an apt application it has to you, to us all who are His epistles!

If you then are an epistle of God, whose Word is of fabulous worth, think how highly He values you, a living expression of the Eternal Logos! Think how careful He will be to preserve you, as He has preserved His written Word throughout the ages. So get off your dusty shelf and let Him pick you up and open you for the edification of the saints and the enlightenment of all men.

YOU ARE A SIGN AND WONDER

You are a *sign* and a potential *wonder!* "Behold I, and the children whom the Lord has given Me are for signs and wonders in Israel from the Lord of Hosts." (Isaiah 8:18) The book of Hebrews records that Jesus quoted this verse, relating it to His followers. And be assured that this includes *you*. The Spirit has often quickened it and impressed it upon us in a very personal way. We are His "sign people" and shall become "wonders" in due season. If we have received the "Mother-Man-child" calling, in each of us too there shall be a fulfillment of the Great Sign in Revelation 12. In us too shall the Man-Child grow up and come forth. If you neglect the nurturing of Christ in yourself, then you shall not likely be made a mother to many. But if, by His grace, the Babe grows to Childhood, and the

Child to a Man, in you, He will see that the Seed is multiplied, and that through His grace in you—by prayer, loving, giving, witnessing and believing—the Seed comes forth in many souls.

How comforting it is to realize that you too may become a chosen "Mother" of and in our Lord. "And stretching out His hand toward (not only the twelve disciples but all) His adherents, He said, 'Here are My mother and My brothers. For whoever does the will of My Father in heaven is My brother and sister and mother!'" (Matthew 12:49,50 Amplified) Another translation reads, "Those who conceive and bear the Word of the Father are My mother, brethren and sisters." Our wonderful Lord will surrender Himself completely to you, even as He placed Himself in the hands of Mary. It is within your power to nurture Him tenderly and faithfully, or to neglect Him, even to abuse Him! Nothing is as helpless as an infant—he is completely so, first in the body, and then in the hands, of his mother. His very helplessness becomes an imperious need. Can you grasp that Jesus *needs you* as vitally and completely *as an infant needs his mother?* This is true! As every mother knows, the coming of a baby requires self-surrender upon her part too. A whole new order begins in her life. Her voice must become gentle and loving, her movements must be quiet and graceful! There is nothing like the handling of a new baby to make a woman feel awkward and rough! She must also clean her house and arrange it for the convenience of the baby. She must see that light, air and warmth are adjusted to his frail little body, for his early struggle to survive is great, and death always stands close by the crib.

The sign of the Woman and Man-child is not the only "wonder" God designs to display in you, though it is a great one. Jesus spoke clearly about "The Sign of the Son of Man," and it is His will to be manifested in each member of His Body as Immanuel, God with us, God in human form. There are also many prophetic signs to be displayed on earth in this latter day. And of course, in due time, there will be the great resurrection of the members of His Body, and their glorification and manifestation in His own beautiful likeness and power.

But even here and now, in your everyday life, you can be a real "demonstrator" for Christ, a sign to point others to Him. As He manifests His grace in you, day by day, you are being made a "spectacle (theatrical or display) to angels and men." (1 Cor. 4:9) In this day when men and women, even children, are engaged in all kinds of demonstrations, displaying all manner of signs for a variety of causes, bear in mind that you too are a sign, designed by Christ to become eventually a *wonder!*

YOU ARE FEARFULLY AND WONDERFULLY MADE

I have long loved Psalm 139, the magnificent Psalm of David that sings of the mystery of our *creation* and *relation* to the Creator. For days the Spirit gave it to me again, in connection with this message about *you*. Then, suddenly, He "seized upon" me to sit down and write it all as a song God sang to David, rather than a song of David to God! I can't put into words the wonder and awe I felt, as the Creator sang this song within my being. May He sing it now to *you*, for He revealed to me that this is His dear desire. (The Spirit referred me to the Amplified and other versions.)

I, the Lord, have searched you thoroughly and known *you*. I know you as you sit and as you rise; I read and understand your thoughts afar off. I sift and search out your path, your walking and your resting, and am acquainted with all your ways. Your life is an open book to Me, for there is not a word in your tongue, though still unuttered, but lo, I, YHVH, know it altogether. I have surrounded you, beset you and shut you in behind and before, and have laid My hand upon you.

Is My infinite knowledge too wonderful for you? Yea, it is far, far beyond you! Where could you go away from My Spirit? Where could you flee from My presence? If you ascend up into heaven, I am there; if you make your bed in Sheol, behold, I am there! If you take the wings of the morning and dwell in the uttermost parts of the sea, even there shall My hand lead you, and My right hand shall hold you. If you say, "Surely the darkness shall cover me, and the night shall cover me with its curtains," even the darkness hides nothing from Me, but the night shines as the day; the darkness and the light are both alike to Me. For I formed your inward parts, I knit you together in your mother's womb.

Praise Me, for I am fearfully wonderful! Praise Me for the wonder of your birth! Wonderful are the works of My creation, and you know it well! Your frame was not hidden from Me, when you were being formed in secret and intricately and curiously wrought in the depths of the earth. My eyes beheld your unformed substance, and *in My book all the days of your life were written, before they took shape,* when as yet there was none of them.

How precious and weighty also are My thoughts of you, I, your God! How vast is the sum of them! If I could count them, they are more in number than the sand. (Imagine this!) And when you awake (in the resurrection?) I will still be with you... I will search you and know your heart. I will try you and know your thoughts. I will see if there is any wicked or hurtful way in you, and lead you in the way everlasting.

Both the mystics and scientists have again and again stressed man's profound ignorance of himself and of the created universe— let alone of God and eternal things. St. Paul likewise declares that even after we have put on Christ and are enlightened of the Spirit, "we see through a glass darkly." "We are looking in a mirror that gives only blurred reflections (of reality as in a riddle or enigma,) but then (when perfection comes) we shall see in reality and face to face! Now you know in part (imperfectly); but then you shall know and understand fully and clearly, even in the same manner as you have been fully and clearly known and understood (by God)." (1 Cor. 13:12, Amplified, using *you* in place of I.)

It is our Lord's desire not only that we confess our faith in the doctrine of the Incarnation, but that we believe it as a *present Truth,* as well as *a historical fact.* "Wherever this doctrine has been denied or hesitatingly taught and believed, it is a fact that purity and chastity have likewise been neglected." So say the Church fathers. The knowledge that Christ is becoming flesh in you—and in me—causes us to sanctify not only our hearts and minds, but our bodies as well, to the honor and glory of God.

How firmly and persistently the Holy Spirit pressed His claims for the sanctification of our physical bodies, as we sought for the Baptism of the Holy Spirit! For what high and holy purposes did He seek this sacrifice! Your body has become the very members of Christ's own Body—His hands, His feet, His heart, His voice!

These lines from Coventry Patmore's writings have been quickened again: "Therefore glorify and bear God in your body... the body is for the Lord and the Lord for the body. That first kiss of God—that baptism of fire which is the tacit knowledge of the Incarnation—is it not a *seal* that God is being made one with your body? The complete satisfaction of God's longing was not attained in the mere *creation* of the human body. It is in His *union* and conjunction with that body that God finds His final perfection and felicity. It is not written that He desires to take hold of the bodies of angels, but of us He has taken hold. The great prophecy, 'Man shall be compassed by a woman,' (Jeremiah 31:22) was fulfilled when Jesus Christ made the body which He had taken from Mary actually divine. The Celestial Marriage was consummated on the Cross. Thenceforward, every soul that chose could participate in such union... No longer think of the Incarnation as a thing of the past only, or a mere figure of speech; learn to know that it consists in your becoming the *intimately* and *humanly* beloved of a Divine and yet human Lover: You are His *local paradise* and *heaven of heavens*."

YOU ARE ACCEPTED IN THE BELOVED

As a fitting climax to this special series concerning *you,* the Holy Spirit has spoken to me strongly in the trenchant, veracious and conciliatory words of our father St. Paul. It was to him that our Lord gave the full and complete revelation of the Ecclesia. It was to him that He entrusted His special instruction for the bride of Christ. And it was Paul who most clearly understood all that is involved in sonship.

Now hear this word, cherished one, *"You are accepted* in the Beloved!" (Ephesians 1:6) *Just as you are,* with all your weaknesses, faults, foolishness and falterings—*you* are not only *acceptable,* but are at this moment fully *accepted* by God the Father, since *you* and your life are hidden away with Christ, the Beloved, in God. (Colossians 3:3) *You* are accepted also by God the Son, for you have been washed in His blood, and He has clothed you with the wedding garment. (Isaiah 61:10) *You* are accepted by God the Spirit, for you have been born again, not of corruptible seed, but of incorruptible. (1 Peter 1:23)

Accepted! For several days this word rang in my heart. I was impressed then to look up the Greek word used here—and I found that it means far more than just to be *accepted!* Charitoo means endued with special honor, highly favored! The Spirit impressed me that most of us have suffered, to some degree at least, from being *unaccepted,* rejected or misunderstood by someone or ones we have loved. It may have been that in childhood we were not fully accepted and loved. Often parents do have difficulty in fully accepting their children—for they find them puzzling, strange and seemingly unlike them. Or it may have been that we knew the heartbreak of unrequited love. This present world has found little in us to accept or desire. And even among the Lord's own people we have each known a little about being unacceptable, cast off, and "without the gate." Whatever we may have suffered—or may still be undergoing—the Spirit made it clear that all that should really matter to us is that Jesus has not only accepted us, but has also found us *desirable!* Let this glorious truth be the "balm of Gilead" that heals all your wounds! And find in His love the acceptance, the fulfillment of your every heart's desire. Remember that all flesh is grass. Cease from man, whose breath is in his nostrils, and let all your expectation and joy be found in the Beloved. All else will pass away or be altered by time. His love abides forever. And His love-union with you will not wane, but wax throughout eternity.

Thus did the Spirit enjoin us: "Because you have been chosen and accepted and embraced so freely by the Lord, without reservation, qualification or equivocation, I beseech *you,* by the love and grace of God, to accept fully and freely all your sisters and brothers in Christ *just as they are,* without criticism, reservation or doubt. Likewise accept your loved ones, your friends, and even *yourself* in the present imperfect, faulty state in which all things in this world exist. Cease to fret and try to change people by your own influence and efforts. You cannot make one hair black or white by your own strength. Moreover, dwelling in the Beloved, accept all circumstances, and all experiences *without resistance or friction,* knowing that God *is* at work continually to cause all things to work together for good for *you*—because you love the Lord and are called according to His purpose. If once you would learn to live *the life of full acceptance,* committing all creatures and conditions to God with fervent prayer and thanksgiving, ceasing from your own thoughts, efforts and words, *great grace* would be manifested in *you.* Then the inevitable tensions of life would be sublimated into power to project you upward and onward to a *higher plane of union and communion with the Beloved.* For, instead of striving with or against your companions, your family, your circumstances—all your striving could be expended on seeking always in all things to live and think and act and speak that which is well-pleasing and acceptable to the Beloved."

Paul also said: "I, Paul, summoned by the will and purpose of God to be an Apostle of Christ Jesus... thank God at all times for *you* because of the grace (the favor and spiritual blessing) of God which was bestowed on *you* in Christ Jesus... He will establish you to the end—keep you steadfast, give you strength, and guarantee your vindication—so that you will be guiltless and irreproachable in the day of our Lord Jesus Christ, the Messiah... I am zealous for *you* with a godly eagerness and a divine jealousy, for I have betrothed *you* to one Husband, to present *you* a chaste virgin to Christ... I appeal to *you*, therefore, and beg you, in view of all the mercies of God, to make a decisive dedication of your bodies—presenting all your members and faculties—as a living (loving) sacrifice, holy and well-pleasing to God, which is your reasonable service and spiritual worship. Do not be conformed to this age, fashioned after and adapted to its external, superficial customs. But be transformed by the (entire) renewal of your mind—so that you may prove what is the good and acceptable and perfect will of God, even the thing which is good and acceptable and perfect (in His sight for you)... Now may the God Who gives the power of patient endurance (steadfastness) and Who supplies encouragement, grant *you* to live in such mutual harmony and such full sympathy with one another, in accord with Christ Jesus, that together you may (unanimously) and with united hearts and one voice, praise and glorify the God and Father of our Lord Jesus Christ, the Messiah.

"In His love He chose *you*—actually picked *you* out for Himself as His own—in Christ before the foundation of the world; that *you* should be holy (consecrated and set apart) and blameless in His sight, even above reproach, before Him in love. For He foreordained *you* (destined you and planned in love for *you*) to be adopted (revealed) as His own son (Greek word: huiothesia—to be *placed as a son*) through Christ Jesus, in accordance with the purpose of His will... In Him *you* have redemption through His blood, the remission of your offences, in accordance with the riches and the generosity of His gracious favor, which He *lavished* upon *you* in every kind of wisdom and understanding, making known to *you* the mystery of His will-of His plan and purpose.

"Christ in *you* is your hope—your earnest and expectation—of glory. As you have received Christ, I urge *you* to walk in Him—regulate your life and conduct yourself in union with and conformity to Him. Have the roots of your being firmly and deeply planted in Him, being continually built up (lifted up) in Him, becoming increasingly more confirmed and established in the faith, just as you were taught, superabounding in it with thanksgiving. *You* are complete in Him, and have come to fulness of life—in Christ *you* too are filled with the Godhead: Father, Son and Holy Spirit—and shall reach full spiritual stature. Therefore, be happy in your faith and rejoice and be glad hearted continually. Thank God in everything—no matter what the circumstances may be, be thankful and give thanks; for this is the will of God for *you* who are in Christ Jesus. Do not quench, suppress or subdue the Holy Spirit. Abstain from all evil. And may the God of peace Himself sanctify *you* through and through—separate *you* from profane things, make *you* pure and wholly consecrated to God—and may your spirit and soul and body be preserved sound and complete and be found blameless at the coming of our Lord Jesus Christ, the Messiah. Faithful is He who has called *you* to Himself, and utterly trustworthy. He will also do it. Amen, so be it." (Quotations taken mainly from the Amplified version.)

The Kingdom of God is within you,
Conceived in your loving heart,
Implanted with God's omnipotent Word
By a flash of His lightning-dart
You are the ground prepared for the seed,
A small plot of dust and clay,
Furrowed and tended by His own hand
For the fruitful latter day.

Your mind has become a castle—
All glorious within—
Set on a hill like a citadel,
And faith is the paladin.
Guard well the hidden treasures of truth,
The wisdom of the prophets and seers,
For you are a small projection
Of the Kingdom, until it appears.

—Frances Metcalfe

THE LIFE THAT SINGS

E. Clementine Schafer

The last tones of the Song faded and, in the awe-filled silence which followed, I knew that I would never be the same. Why? Because a Song—or, was it the Singer?—had captured my heart. This beautiful Prayer-Song had always thrilled *me,* but never before had it made such a deep impression upon *me.* It was more than an emotional thrill—it was a sublime experience, one that I shall never forget.

Who can express with finite words the effect which music has upon us? Carlyle says music is "A kind of inarticulate, unfathomable speech, which leads us to the edge of the infinite, and lets us for moments gaze into that!" We are affected by its power, but know not *why*—unless we believe what the poet has said: "God is its Author, and not man; He laid the key-note of all harmonies; He planned all perfect combinations, and *He made us so that we could hear and understand.*"

"Music is the atmosphere of Heaven," it is said. In that supernal realm myriad angelic beings voice their praise to God Most High with "sweet, incessant songs." Music is also universal, present everywhere. Our own amazing earth came into being to the accompaniment of celestial melody.

"Where were you," God asked the patriarch Job, "when I laid the foundations of the earth?... Upon what were the foundations of it fastened, or who laid its cornerstone, when the morning stars sang together, and the sons of God (angels) shouted for joy?" (Job 38:4-7; Amplified)

The Amplified adds an interesting and enlightening note: "For centuries this statement, 'the morning stars sang together,' was accepted as a mere figure of speech; but now we know that a beam of light can be transformed into sound waves revealing each individual star's 'song.'" Which, of course, we can hear only in fancy. But God has made us so that we *can* hear and enjoy the music that is pulsating all around us. The magic of bird-songs, the carefree melody of brook and stream, and the song of the wind as it plays on the harp of a thousand strings, are but a few measures in Nature's Symphony that shall never cease to thrill us.

And the Bible! Who has read it and never felt the charm of its music? Page after page of the holy Book is an Album of Sacred Music—the inspired songs of God's people in ages past. With a little imagination we can "tune in" and listen to Israel's Temple Choir singing the Psalms of David. Hear the men, their voices deep and strong, proclaiming Jehovah's honor and strength! And the women, in antiphony clear and high, singing the beauty of His holiness! Listen to the immortal songs of Moses and Miriam, of Deborah and Barak, the Songs of Solomon, of Hannah, of Elizabeth, and of Mary! Songs out of the past, yet timeless, universal! Songs of incomparable beauty, magnificent hymns of praise, that have inspired worshipers through the centuries to sing praises to God our King!

THE SINGER AND THE SONG

Now let me tell you my story. One afternoon I lay down to rest; however, before I could get comfortably settled, and to my utter surprise, suddenly I sensed the nearness of the Holy Spirit, and heard Someone *singing*. I heard The Song within me, but it was not I who was singing it. I knew I was lying on a couch; yet, strangely, it seemed that I was sitting in a sanctuary, listening to a tenor Soloist singing Malotte's "The Lord's Prayer."

I knew intuitively there was a message in The Song, so I silently worshiped and listened expectantly, drinking in every word. Every word, every syllable, from "Our Father" to the "Amen" was vibrant, alive. My spirit seemed to be a living, sensitized instrument upon which The Song was indelibly impressed. And when the singing ended, my heart fervently echoed the "Amen."

I cannot say how long I was held in the power of the blessed stillness that followed. Then I became aware that The Song was being "played back," and when the phrase *"Thy kingdom come; Thy will be done, in earth, as it is in heaven"* was sung, I knew this was it— *this was the message* I had expected. This phrase came alive with new meaning, moving me in the depths of my being in an indescribable way. I felt the words searching my heart, discerning my thoughts, probing, questioning...

"Thy kingdom come..." I had always related this event to the future when Christ reigns on earth during the Millennium. But *now* I knew that before His visible reign begins on earth, there is an invisible enthronement of Him as King—here and now, in your heart and mine.

For some time the Holy Spirit tenderly and insistently pressed the claims of Christ's lordship in my life; and I knew it was time for spiritual inventory—time for earnest heart-searching. Am I honestly yielding the scepter to His dear Hand? Does He rule in every area of my life, or are there "reserved" areas I am not aware of? Does Christ truly have control in my work, my pleasures, plans, habits, time—everything? Deeper and deeper went the search, into the subtle area of Self with its traits and dispositions. In the light of the Word, the picture I saw of myself, though one of contrition, was certainly not a radiant one.

"Thy will be done..." The music continued—filling the air, enveloping me, surging through my being in healing, cleansing waves, melting my heart with an unutterable longing to become lost in the will of God; a longing to know the blessed release of abandonment to His will, not in part of my life some of the time, but all of my life all the time.

"In earth..." I wondered why the message was coming to me in a Song. "*I want you to be My Song—in the earth,*" was the surprising reply. Suddenly, my heart thrilled with understanding. The Christian's life *is a Song,* if it is lived in harmony with God's will! Not a life of discord, lived on the level of self-will, of fear and duty, of doubts and defeat, but the radiant, triumphant *life of faith and praise. The life that sings!*

Some time later, I learned that St. Ignatius, centuries ago, had beautifully expressed this thought in one of his letters to the Christians: "Therefore in your concord and agreeing charity, *Jesus Christ is sung...*" How true! Wherever Jesus Christ is sung by believers who are in "concord and agreeing charity" others are influenced and transformed by the power of His love. I was saddened by the thought that there are still countless thousands who have never heard, multitudes who are listening for His Song in the earth.

"Thy kingdom come, Thy will be done..." For several weeks the music haunted me. Day after day The Song rang in my heart, and frequently I heard it played or sung by others. Invariably, when this particular phrase was sung, I felt a pathos in the words that wrung my heart and melted me to tears—tears of contrition for my failures and shortcomings, and tears of longing in my heart "to be His Song."

LEARNING TO BE HIS SONG

And there were also tears of joyful surrender! I am now enrolled in the Master's Singing Class, and the Singer Himself is the Teacher.

"Remember always," He says, *"the life that sings* is a life in harmony with the will of God." Soberly I have contemplated His words, and realize that if my life is to be His Song, many changes will be necessary. The "strings" of my heart will have to be tuned again and again—it takes so little to get them out of tune! And I shall have to learn the "rudiments of music," and practice faithfully.

We are now practicing exercises in "attunement"—learning to know the promptings and checks of the Holy Spirit; learning to be still and to listen for His gentle whispers, and many other such things. Although it is easier now to sing *"Thy* will" instead of *"my* will," something is still lacking! When the Teacher sings "Thy will be done," His voice thrills with the spirit of utter and loving abandonment to the will of God. The will of God is His joy, His delight! Oh, how different it sounds when I try to sing it. My voice is thin, quavering, uncertain.

"No, no, no!" the Master says, "This is the way." Over and over He sings the phrase to show how it should be done. "My child, *doing the will of God is good, but not good enough. If you would be His Song, you must delight in His will.* This will be your next lesson."

So I called the exercise, "Delighting-to-do-the-will-of-God," and began to practice enthusiastically. For a little while it was fairly easy, then the novelty began to wear off; the exercises became more difficult as the trials increased, and my enthusiasm waned. Singing with delight was more difficult than I had thought. Besides, I soon discovered that my "singing exercises" were very trying to those around me.

By this time I was tempted to despair, for I seemed to be getting nowhere. The Teacher patiently encouraged me and quoted something which another had learned, which I'll never forget: "Never despair; but if you do, work on in despair!" So I continued practicing and suddenly, happily, my singing noticeably improved. It was getting easier "to delight."

PRACTICE...

In this life we shall never be done with *practice.* Slight it, and we shall invariably revert to our incorrect habits; neglect it, and the Teacher will know it, we shall know it, and soon everyone around us will know it—our Song will be off-key!

Learning to be His Song requires *discipline:* the discipline of *self-denial, patience, perseverance,* and *humility.*

Self-denial is one of the first things you and I must learn if we would sing Jesus Christ. "If anyone desires to be My disciple," Jesus said, "let him deny himself—that is disregard, lose sight of and forget himself and his interests—and take up his cross and follow Me..." (Matthew 16:24; Amplified)

The desires and interests of Self do indeed conflict with the will of God. But, does this mean that self-denial will condemn us to a life of misery? Never! Self-love makes us shrink from the will of God because we fear it will make us unhappy. Are we more concerned about happiness than holiness? "Seek happiness for its own sake," said Tyron Edwards, "and you will not find it; seek for duty, and happiness will follow as the shadow comes with the sunshine." Another has wisely said, "Happiness is neither within us only, or without us; *it is the union of ourselves with God.*" The heart in union with God can sing, "Sweet will of God still fold me closer till I am wholly lost in Thee..."

"Let *patience* have her perfect work," St. James said. If anyone can bear pains, trials and adversities without complaining, he has patience. We should not, however, mistake sullen endurance for patience. "Patience strengthens the spirit and sweetens the temper." There is a Chinese proverb which says, "Patience is power; with time and patience the mulberry leaf becomes silk." So too, with time and patience our unlovely lives can become a Song!

Perseverance gets the work done. Nothing is performed with ease that was not practiced with perseverance. We usually begin a new venture with exuberance and excitement; but when these wane, as they always do, we learn the value of stick-to-itiveness. Many individuals with only ordinary ability succeed by steadfastly pursuing their aim in life; while others with far greater potential fail because they lack perseverance. I like Longfellow's verse about perseverance: "The divine insanity of noble minds, that never falters nor abates, but labors, endures, and waits, till all that it foresees it finds, or what it cannot find, creates."

"*Humility*—that low, sweet root, from which all heavenly virtues shoot," said the poet. This virtue teaches us that we are not sufficient of ourselves—that our sufficiency is found only in God. We shall not have practiced long before we learn that human effort alone cannot bring success in a divine endeavor. All who would live the life that sings must depend upon "Him who humbled Himself by living a life of utter obedience to His Father." (Phil. 2:5,8; Phillips) Can we comprehend the depth of Christ's humility? "Let this... humble mind be in you which was in Christ Jesus—let Him be your example in humility—Who, although being essentially one with God and in the form of God... stripped Himself... so as to assume the guise of a servant (slave), in that He became like men and was born a human being... and carried His obedience to the extreme of death, even the death of the cross!" (Phil. 2:5,8; Amplified)

"Should you ask me," said St. Augustine, "'What is the first thing in religion?' I should reply, 'The first, second and third thing therein—nay, all—is humility.'"

Oh, let us thank God for every thing that lays our pride and self-sufficiency low in the dust. God grant that our weaknesses and failures will teach us to lean harder on Him who said, "Learn of Me, for I am gentle and humble in heart."

...AND MORE PRACTICE

Desire to be His Song should be the only incentive needed to keep us practicing. However, human nature being weak, we tend to shirk. Just remembering the pain of our past failures will help prod our sluggish spirits into action. Do you remember when the ugly sound of discord began to come into your life? I well remember *my* sad experience. We were often gloomy and dejected, and wondered why we didn't "have the blessing." Where was the delight we once knew, the reality of His presence, the sweetness of communion with our Lord? Where had we failed? Then the light began to dawn. Mother Eve "got out of tune" because she listened to the voice of the Deceiver and let doubt, discontent and ambition enter her heart. And experienced to her sorrow the bitterness of broken fellowship with her God. Oh, how diligently we turn again to our lessons!

At times when the going gets rough, we are prone to forget that life isn't always easy. What then? Lapse into our old ways and indulge in a little self-pity? Become depressed, discouraged? Or perhaps murmur and complain? And neglect our Song?

Our Teacher tells us what to do when we encounter tests and trials: "Consider it wholly joyful..." (James 1:2) And we hear the measured tick of the metronome and the rhythmic beat of our heart echo His words: "Whol-ly joy-ful... whol-ly joy-ful... whol-ly joy-ful..." "You will not always *feel* joyful," He says: "you must *consider* the trials joyful because they are sent for a purpose—for the trial and proving of your faith." We soon found this to be true. Our task isn't accomplished by "*feel*"-ing, but by "*will*"-ing. Does one go to his daily work only when he feels like it? Neither can we learn our Song by practicing only when we feel like it.

"The *will* is the governing power in man's nature," said A.B. Simpson; "if the will *is* set right, all the rest of nature must come into harmony." This includes our *attitude*. If our attitude about doing

God's will is one of grim resolution, as something to be endured, our Song will be dismal and flat. Our attitude, in turn, determines our *altitude*. We must get off the ground, and climb high, *if we would sing!*

THE LIFE OF FAITH AND PRAISE

Training in any field of endeavor has its price. *Learning to sing Jesus Christ* is most costly, but not in terms of perishable silver and gold. The tuition fee for this training is the precious *gold of faith*. Faith is the basic principle, the first essential, for the Christian life. There can be no contact with God without faith. "But without faith it is impossible to please and be satisfactory to Him. For whoever would come near to God must necessarily believe that God exists and that He is the Rewarder of those who earnestly and diligently seek Him out." (Hebrews 11:6; Amplified)

You and I have a measure of faith; but is it enough for the radiant, triumphant life? Faith for *the life that sings* must be strong enough to meet the challenge of life and to *triumph* in the conflict; it must be strong enough to stand the test victoriously, *joyfully.*

Trouble and suffering are universal. The whole world suffers; not because it is God's will, but because of sin and evil introduced into the world by the fall of Adam. All around us there is abject misery and wretchedness—troubles too numerous to count, troubles that seem more than human spirit can endure. No one is exempt: the guilty suffer, likewise the innocent. Troubles often befall us without our being personally or directly the cause of them. "One half the world is busy making the other half miserable" was perhaps said facetiously, but it is true.

How does suffering fit into God's plan for the Christian—for those who would be His Song? In His infinite love and wisdom, God *uses* suffering as a school of training. When Adam and Eve were tested, they failed. And ever since the human race has suffered. Jesus, the Second Adam, passed His test "more than a conqueror." *He shows us how to overcome.* "In the world you have tribulation and trials and distress and frustration," He said; "but be of good cheer—take courage, be confident, certain, undaunted—for I have overcome the world—I have deprived it of power to harm, have conquered it for you." (John 16:33; Amplified)

Suffering *of itself*, however, cannot perfect our faith or change our natures. Multitudes are suffering who have become bitter and resentful—they suffer in vain. We see there must be a yielding, an acceptance, on our part, with *faith* and *humility.*

Since Jesus has told us that tribulation and trials are inevitable, why should we lose heart and become discouraged? There are times when everything seems to go wrong—we're all familiar with the experience. Suddenly the sun hides his face, storm clouds gather, and before we know it we are deluged with a flood of trouble beyond our control that threatens to overwhelm us.

When trials come, as they surely do, *what is our reaction?* (Remember, Jesus did not promise *exemption* from trouble; He said trouble could not *harm* us.) Many and various are the individual's reaction to trouble. Some question and doubt; many murmur and complain of their lot in life; some sink into Bunyan's "slough of despond;" others rebuke the devil and demand deliverance— immediately; some blame the Lord and become rebellious; still others faint with despair. There are also those who really believe that "all things work together for good"—who submit to "the will of God" with grim resolution, but fail to triumph in the test. Which class are you and I in? I'm sure all of us at times have reacted in a similar way. And this is *not* the way to *sing Jesus Christ! This is not the life of faith and praise!*

Since we are a part of humanity, we may be sure that so long as we live we are going to have trouble. Centuries ago, Job made this observation: "Man that is born of a woman is of few days, and full of trouble." This fact alone convinces us that we need *faith*—strong faith, stronger than many of us now have. Friends, are you having difficulty rising above the problems of life? Are you often "grounded" by a faith that is too weak? *Would you like to know how your faith can be fortified?*

It is an "open secret." The answer is clear and plain in the Word; but it seems to have evaded us, or perhaps we have evaded it. Today, many of God's people are learning this "secret." They are learning the power of PRAISE—*the blessing of praising God in all circumstances.* And their lives are being marvelously transformed. And like the eagles, they are soaring into the "heights," and are renewing their strength. But of course *wings* are necessary for this flight—*two* wings—the wings of FAITH and PRAISE ! Yes, friends, PRAISE is the *other wing*, the companion of FAITH. Praise gives the extra *lift* we need to rise above the cares and troubles of life.

Would you be *strong in faith*? Be *strong in praise*! When we think of faith we usually think of Abraham, who "was *strong in faith*, giving glory to God." (Romans 4:20) Early one morning just as I awoke, the Holy Spirit spoke this word to my heart: "Give glory to God, and be strong in faith." I was puzzled, for I knew it was Romans 4:20, in reverse. So I looked at several other translations and found to my surprise and delight that they clearly set forth the idea that *faith is strengthened as we praise*. The Amplified says: "But he (Abram) grew strong and *was empowered by faith as he gave glory to God.*" Williams: "Yet he never staggered in doubt at the promise of God but *grew strong in faith, because he gave glory to God.*" Moffat: "No unbelief made him waver about God's promise; *his faith won strength as he gave glory to God...*" My heart simply overflowed with praise, and a little chorus came to me:

When father Abram received the promise,
He bowed and worshiped the Lord;
Doubting and fear gave place to praises—
His faith grew strong in God's Word.

Then keep on praising the Lord, my heart,
Keep on praising the Lord;
Rejoice and give thanks in every thing,
And keep on praising the Lord.

SINGING WITH THE SAINTS

Would you be strong in faith? Be strong in praise! We have inherited a lovely treasury of Song, a repertory of precious Psalms of Praise. Though the voices of the singers were stilled on earth long ago, their songs have lived on. May the Holy Spirit use these Songs of Faith and Praise to stir our hearts and inspire us to sing *our* Song!

In the fire of tragedy and physical pain, the patriarch Job's immortal Song was born. No doubt you've already learned to sing this familiar refrain: "The Lord gave, and the Lord hath taken away; *blessed be the name of the Lord!*" (Job 1:21; also, Job 23:10)

The prophet Habakkuk's Song is a classic paean of Faith and Praise. He declared that even though the fruit of their fields, their orchards and their flocks should utterly fail, he would still praise the Lord: "*Yet I will rejoice, I will joy in the God of my salvation!*" (Hab. 3:17-19)

Through Faith and Praise Judah won a great victory over the invading enemy host. We read, "Jehoshaphat appointed *singers* unto the Lord to go out before the army and *to praise the beauty of holiness, and to say, Praise the Lord; for His mercy endureth forever.*" (2 Chr. 20)

Take for example also the holy apostles. How did *they* react in time of tribulation and trouble? Listen to the Song of Paul and Silas: in an inner prison, their backs beaten and bleeding, their feet fast in stocks, these soldiers of the Cross exultantly *sang praises unto God!*

No wonder the Saints can teach us how to rejoice! Paul's words fairly sing: "I am *exceeding joyful* in all our tribulations... *Rejoice evermore...* In every thing *give thanks...* We *glory* in tribulation also... I *take pleasure* in infirmities, in reproaches, in necessities, in persecutions, in distresses for Christ's sake." (2 Cor. 7:4; 1 Thess. 5:16-19; Romans 5:3; 2 Cor. 12:10)

Hear the triumphant shout in Peter's voice as he *glorifies the Lord:* "Beloved, think it not strange concerning the fiery trial which is to try you, as though some strange thing happened unto you: but *rejoice...* Yet if any man suffer as a Christian... let him *glorify God* on this behalf." (1 Peter 1:6; 4:12,16)

The apostle James' word really challenges our faith: "When all kinds of trials and temptations crowd into your lives, my brothers, *don't resent them as intruders but welcome them as friends!*" (James 1:2; Phillips) The Authorized says: "My brethren, *count it all joy...*" The Amplified: "*Consider it wholly joyful...*" Williams: "You must consider it the *purest joy...*" Moffatt: "*Greet it as pure joy...*" Whichever translation we accept, I confess it presents a mighty challenge to *my* faith!

I cannot close this chapter on "Singing with the Saints" until we hear what our Lord Jesus says: "Blessed are you when people hate you and exclude you and denounce you, and spurn your name as evil, for the sake of the Son of Man. *Burst into joy* on that day and *leap for ecstacy,* for your reward will be rich in heaven..." (Luke 6:23; Williams)

PRAISE—THE AFFIRMATION OF FAITH

Praise is the affirmation of faith. Praise *declares*, *affirms* and *asserts our faith in God*—in His nature, in all His works and ways.

True praise is not mere *form* or *ritual*. It is not the *mechanical repetition of words*—it is the spontaneous overflow of praise from the heart. True praise glorifies God, not self. Praise gives God the vote of confidence; it tells Him that we *believe Him*, we *trust Him*, we *love Him*—even though our petitions may be delayed or denied, for "He doeth all things well."

Praise affirms all this and more, much more. This is what praise means to me:

PRAISE IS FAITH IN ACTION

Praise is faith resolving discord, awakening harmony;
> Praise is faith singing a joyous symphony;
Praise is faith smiling through your tears;
> Praise is faith trusting in the barren years;
Praise is faith triumphing in the trials;
> Praise is faith accepting God's denials;
Praise is faith routing the foe;
> Praise is faith declaring "I know it's so;"
Praise is faith overcoming blunders;
> Praise is faith working wonders;
Praise is faith counting unseen blessings;
> Praise is faith God's Word confessing;
Praise is faith piercing the dark;
> Praise is faith hitting the mark;
Praise is faith leaning on God's arm;
> Praise is faith banishing alarm;

> Praise is faith seizing the prize;
> Praise is faith soaring to the skies;
> Praise is faith shouting the victory;
> Praise is for TIME and for ETERNITY!

PRAISE—AN EXPERIENCE

Would you be His Song? Prove the power of praise. Know by experience that praise will fortify your faith. Draw near to God in praise—praise Him by faith for everything, in everything; praise Him for a whole day—for a week—two weeks—and on and on and on. At times your praises may be only a whisper; at times they may spring up and overflow like a geyser. They need not always be audible; it may be only the lifting up of the heart to God; but let it be fervent, constant, sincere. No matter how tried and tested you may be, purpose to sing *your* Song of Faith and Praise. You will be surprised and thrilled at the result of this experiment in praise.

Would you be His Song? "Yes! But there is so much confusion in life," you say, "so much that is hard to understand." You don't have to *understand* God's ways; only *believe* Him. St. Paul said, "And we do know that all things work together for good to them that love God, who are the called according to His purpose." (Romans 8:28) Oh, what a bulwark for our faith ! Friend, take hold of this Word and believe it!

God is saying here the very things that are happening to you *now* are fitting into His plan. These very things, the "all things," are the intangibles *your* Song is made of. When the tests come, *use them.* Make them the theme of your Song. Don't wait until the trial is over; believe God, and praise Him without delay. Delay, even for a moment, can open the door for a host of doubts and fears that will weaken your faith and silence your Song.

Don't waste time and dissipate faith by blaming people and circumstances for the troubles that befall you; they are God's instruments for your refining—by His own choosing. See His blessed Hand in the "all things;" admit to no "second cause."

"To rejoice in God's will when that will imparts nothing but happiness," said Madame Guyon, "is easy even for the natural man. But no one but the renovated man can rejoice in the Divine will when it crosses his path, disappoints his expectations, and overwhelms him with sorrow."

And St. Paul said, "Be filled with the Spirit; converse with one another in the music of psalms, in hymns, and in songs of the spiritual life, praise the Lord heartily with words and music, and render thanks to God the Father in the name of Jesus Christ at all times, and for all things." (Ephesians 5: 19; Moffatt)

The power of praise is beyond all knowing. New facets of its beauty and power are brought into view before our wondering eyes every day. Yes, my friend, it works!

A SONG NO ONE ELSE CAN SING

Does your life seem humdrum, commonplace? Are you tempted to think your life counts for little or nothing? Let me tell you a secret: you and I have a Song that no one else can sing! What if we should fail to sing it? You did try for a while, you say, but thought it didn't amount to much; you got discouraged and gave up. Don't you know Satan hates your Song, and that he will do all he can to silence it? When we fail to sing our Song of faith and praise, discord enters. Martin Luther said, "Music is one of the fairest and most glorious gifts of God, to which Satan is a bitter enemy."

David, the "sweet psalmist of Israel," began singing his Song when he was just a youth while tending his father's sheep—long before he became famous for the slaying of Goliath; long before he was anointed King of Israel. In the heat of day and the chill of night, in the solitude of plain and hill, he played his harp and lifted his voice in praise to Jehovah. To David's inspired heart, each experience became the theme for a song of praise. Every act, every deed, was a new stanza in his Song. Is it any wonder that David's songs have never died? What a loss to us had David never learned his Song of Praise!

Of course there won't be another David. But even the most ordinary life can be translated into a most extraordinary Song—your song and mine. So, if your life is dull and uneventful, and you long for holy Adventure, *sing your Song. Begin now!* Faith and Praise will transpose the discord in your life to paeans of victory and blessing that you never dreamed possible.

Would you be His Song? "My heart is too heavy to sing," you reply. My friend, the heart that *sings Jesus Christ* will know pain—intimately. Are you fainting beneath a load of care? *Use your wings of faith and praise!* You will find your strength renewed—you too will "run and not be weary, and walk and not faint." He who fainteth not, neither is weary, gives power to the faint!

Do floods of trouble overwhelm your soul? Offer the *praise of faith*—it is music to God's ears. And hear Him saying to your heart, "When thou passest through the waters I will be with thee; and through the rivers, they shall not overflow thee."

Is your heart breaking with sorrow? Praise Him, dear one, even through your tears. A poet has said, "The soul would have no rainbow had the eyes no tears." Remember, our Lord was a "man of sorrows and acquainted with grief," and He alone knows how to mend broken hearts. (Psa. 147:3)

Oh, friends, if you would see the glory of the Lord revealed, let *your* Song and Sacrifice ascend together, a sweet incense unto our

God. (2 Chron. 29:27) There is no song more acceptable, no incense sweeter unto Him.

LESSONS IN HARMONY

Our Singing Class is humming these days with activity and excitement. The Teacher has told us that all who would live *the life that sings* must *learn how to sing with others!* So we are now taking an intensive course in Harmony, and having Choir practice by the hour. Our assignment is the beautiful Composition called "The More Excellent Way," an arrangement by Saint Paul. Our Teacher says this Composition is the End, the Ultimate, and that it has been recognized as the "Song Perfect" by singers of every generation. The theme of the Composition is *divine love.* No work has ever been composed that is comparable to it. The Score is arranged for full Chorus; therefore, we are digging deep into the mysteries and intricacies of Harmony.

We can hardly wait until we learn our parts; but at present, the Teacher keeps us constantly practicing difficult exercises. Very solemnly He tells us that it is not possible to sing *this* Song until we learn how to harmonize; and this can be done by one method only—the one taught by Master Paul.

Each one in the Class has a copy of these exercises which we have come to know as "First Corinthians Thirteen," so called, because they were first written for the Church at Corinth. Being a Master in Music, Saint Paul's instructions are complete in every detail: he has omitted nothing; and his technique is simply superb. In a truly convincing and eloquent style he compares the exercises of divine love with other Methods.

You see, there were some in the Church at Corinth in those days who were carried away with the exercises of certain gifts and abilities which without doubt were very important but which, in themselves, did not make for *harmony*. The Corinthians had neglected the exercises of divine love, and as a result there was much discord in their "music." Saint Paul was very much concerned about this unhappy unharmonious situation, therefore he introduced "The More Excellent Way," with special exercises designed to produce beautiful harmony. Saint Paul pointed out many undeniable facts, and proved that practicing these exercises was better by far than other methods in achieving harmony. Have you ever heard an argument more beautiful, eloquent, and convincing?

"I may speak with the tongues of men and of angels, but if I have no love, I am a noisy gong or a clanging cymbal;

"I may prophesy, fathom all mysteries and secret lore, I may have such absolute faith that I can move hills from their place, but if I have no love, I count for nothing;

"I may distribute all I possess in charity, I may give up my body to be burnt, but if I have no love, I make nothing of it."

In this comparison you will notice that Master Paul does not depreciate ecstatic tongues, prophecy, faith, etc.; nor does he speak disparagingly of their practice. He does, however, emphasize the fact that these are *valueless* without divine love. He then continues in the defense of "The More Excellent Way" and defines its theme in language unmistakably plain.

"Love is very patient, very kind,
Love knows no jealousy;
Love makes no parade,

Gives itself no airs,
Is never rude, never selfish,
Never irritated, never resentful;

"Love is gladdened by goodness,
Always slow to expose,
Always eager to believe the best,
Always hopeful, always patient.
Love never disappears." (1 Cor. 13; Moffatt)

Our Teacher explained Saint Paul's method very carefully, and convinced us there is no other way to achieve harmony with others. We have paraphrased the first paragraph of the lesson, and made it our motto:

"I may *sing* with the tongues of men and of angels, but if I have no love, my *song* is a noisy gong or a clanging cymbal."

We keep the motto close by and read it often, for this is the *key* to Harmony. We are told that all singers have difficulty mastering these lessons, and it is no wonder!

If the exercises are not diligently practiced, the singers' voices are noticeably affected, often becoming very unmusical and off-key; sometimes harsh and rough, with a jarring, grating quality. No one with a voice like this can *sing Jesus Christ!*

There are still times when the discord of self and sin is manifest in our midst, despite all our practice. Oh, how this grieves our Teacher! Patiently He reiterates the importance, the absolute necessity, of harmony. Chastened and humbled, we practice more faithfully, and soon the discord is resolved in peace and understanding, in beautiful heart-warming fellowship, and sweet communion of spirit with spirit. Oh, how good, how pleasant it is when we *sing in harmony!*

Master Paul also composed other excellent exercises in Harmony. This one is very effective when practiced: "So, if there is any appeal in our union with Christ, if there is any persuasive power in love... fill up my cup of joy by living in harmony, by fostering the same disposition of love, your hearts beating in unison, your minds set on one purpose." (Phil. 2:2; Williams)

With Saint Paul, we can say, "I count not myself to have apprehended; but this one thing I do... I press toward the mark!"

ON EARTH—AS IT IS IN HEAVEN

"PRAISE is the work and happiness of Heaven," writes Matthew Henry, "and all who would go to Heaven hereafter, must begin their heaven now. We praise God, and give Him glory, not because He needs it, but because He deserves it."

"One of the most essential preparations for eternity," says Thomas Chalmers, "is delight in praising God; a higher delight, I do think, than even delight and devotedness in prayers."

Our Song of Praise on earth is the Prelude of the Music of Heaven. In that glorious Realm, the voices of the heavenly Ones are melodious with praise; there is not a single note of discord—all is harmony. Discord on this earth is the result of unresolved self and sin. Have you ever wondered what others would *hear* if our every thought, word and deed were transposed into *sound*? A sober thought, indeed.

Our Song cannot be learned in a few easy lessons—a lifetime is required, for it is Life's Song, born of faith, polished in the fires of tribulation, and made sweeter because of pain.

Your Song, my Song, is unique; no one else can sing it. Every hour of every day we must practice it and rehearse for the Day when we shall sing together with the Choir of Heaven. Then shall our little "parts" blend harmoniously in one glorious "whole." (1 Cor. 13:9,10)

Would you be His Song? H.G. Lewes said, "Character is built out of circumstances—from exactly the same materials one builds palaces, while another builds hovels." Likewise our Song of Faith and Praise is composed of exactly the same materials available to everyone—the total experience of life. The beauty of our Song depends upon *how we use* these materials.

Oh, friends, it will take more than a lifetime to explore the power of Praise. Its possibilities are measured by our faith—the "faith that worketh by love." Who has known its height, depth, breadth and length?

Praise strengthens the sinews of faith.

Heartfelt praise opens the windows of Heaven, and opens our eyes to see beyond the "smog" of this world.

Praise delivers us from depression and gloom, and scatters the powers of darkness more quickly than long praying.

Our hearts are warmed with God's love, our spirits are sweetened by His grace, when we practice true praise.

Praise breaks through *all* barriers—sound, time and space—into the dimension of Infinity.

Our burdens are lighter, our day is brighter, when our hearts overflow with praise.

Praise brings down "the walls of Jericho"—the walls of enmity and opposition.

Praise tunes out the discord of life—attunes us in harmony with the Divine will.

Praise becomes "The Lost Chord" when we are out of harmony with God.

Are we praisers or beggars? What is our favorite refrain?—"Lord, bless me," or "Lord, I bless Thee."

Unless we become more familiar with the language of praise, we may feel like a stranger when we get to Heaven.

Praise is an irresistible magnet that unites the soul and God.

Nothing is as fulfilling in this brief life as practicing the presence of God in praise.

Dear soul, are you "prayed-out," utterly exhausted, and still feel no touch from the Lord? Try changing your prayers to praises!

Lay your weary head upon the Father's breast and tell Him that you love Him, trust Him, and praise Him, even though you can't see or understand the way He is leading.

Would you be His Song? When circumstances seem the darkest, when the pressures and stresses of life seem unbearable, when despair threatens to overwhelm you, open wide your heart to God in *faith;* then open wide your mouth and *sing His praise!*

You don't think anyone could praise God, actually sing praise, under such circumstances? The saints did! And there are multitudes today who are discovering the power of praise to strengthen faith and lift them above the cares of earth.

God has promised "beauty for ashes, the oil of joy for mourning, and the garment of praise for the spirit of heaviness." (Isa. 61:3) How? If we will only *believe Him* and *humble ourselves* under His mighty Hand, He will do the rest. By the miracle of divine alchemy, our deepest sorrows, our greatest losses, are transformed into blessing—blessing "exceeding abundantly above all we can ask or think..."

I know this to be true. And, dear friends, many of you know it. God demonstrates this miracle again and again as we sing our Song of Faith and Praise. Tragedy is turned into triumph, and sorrow into singing! We don't know *how* God does it; we only know *He does!*

How can we express the inexpressible love and blessing which God bestows upon all who, by His grace, practice praise! Oh, that we would abandon ourselves to God in fervent praise—*not for personal blessing and favors,* but because we love and trust Him. And, above all, because He is God, a great and good God, and worthy of our most fervent praise!

God cannot resist those who come to Him with loving adoration and thankful praise. The blessings He gives far outweigh all our trials and burdens. "According to His riches in glory by Christ Jesus," is the measure of His bounty toward us. "Exceeding abundantly above all we can ask or think," and "Good measure, pressed down, heaped up, and running over," are a couple more of the yardsticks of our Father's generosity.

Yes, He simply overwhelms us with blessing. Visions of "the things which He has prepared for them that love Him," glimpses of Truth which unshackles the soul, flashes of His Shekinah, foretastes of the delights of Paradise, and countless other tokens of His love and grace are bestowed upon His thankful children.

In His gracious presence, living fountains spring up in the thirsty ground of our spirits; our wilderness becomes a fruitful garden; and our raptured hearts sing with gladness:

> Oh, my heart is now a garden
> That blooms and sings for joy;
> It's a garden of delight,
> Where the skies are blue and bright,
> In God's Paradise of Love.

Oh, friends, the life of faith and praise is not *all* testing and tribulation. Again and again we are invited into the Master's garden where He communes with us heart-to-heart. We feast at His table and partake of the wine of His love, and we are refreshed. A single hour in His hallowed presence banishes our cares, and we should like to stay in His presence forever. But we are not permitted to remain long in this paradise and enjoy the foretaste of heaven's bliss.

For, while we are enjoying the fellowship of our Lord, something wonderful happens. Our eyes are opened to see His great Heart; we feel His Love that embraces the whole world—His arms opened wide to receive "whosoever will." We sense His longing to resolve the discord of every troubled soul, His desire to make them His Song. And He imparts to us the desire to share His Love—to tell others about His transforming power.

Oh, friends, you and I have rich blessings to share—let us share them! We have a Song to sing—let us sing it! For who can tell how many hearts will hear and respond, and rejoice?

TAXES OR TRIBUTE

Frances Metcalfe

TAXES OR TRIBUTE

Search out the golden coin of your heart and read
That which is clearly stamped or written there,
Search out the golden coin of your heart and see—
Whose image and superscription does it bear?

Caesar's? Then render to him his rightful tax.
God's? Withhold not that which belongs to God.
Pay tax or tribute unto the powers you serve
Whether they be of the fasces or of the Rod.

If the prince of this present world is your god and lord,
Bow down your soul to his cruel exacting ways;
But if your allegiance is unto the King of Kings,
Then render to Him full tribute of highest praise!

—Frances Metcalfe

TAXES OR TRIBUTE

Ａnd it came to pass in those days, that there went out a decree from Caesar Augustus, that all the world should be taxed... And all went to be taxed, everyone unto his own city. And Joseph also went up from Galilee, out of the city of Nazareth, into Judea unto the city of David, which is called Bethlehem: (because he was of the house and lineage of David:) to be taxed with Mary, his espoused wife, being great with child. And so it was, that, while they were there, the days were accomplished that she should be delivered. And she brought forth her first-born son, and wrapped him in swaddling clothes, and laid him in a manger; because there was no room for them in the inn."

Thus it was that the event for which Israel had waited through the centuries came at a time when it lay broken and crushed beneath the Oppressor's heel. The Devourer had despoiled the nations. The Exactor was now claiming his due. The prince of this world, through Rome, had levied a cruel tax upon the chosen people of God. The kingdom of David, of which such glorious prophecies had been spoken, lay in the dust. Instead of wielding the promised scepter, Judah's back was bowed down under the authority of the hated fasces. Why, Jerusalem itself—crown city of God—was defiled by the horsemen and chariots of a heathen ruler! Nor did God, in His mercy, miraculously deliver the faithful remnant of Israel out of the hands of their enemies. They paid the same tax of suffering and substance—if not a greater one—that the rebellious and unfaithful of their race.

Contrary to the belief of many well-meaning children of God, divine election and favor has never exempted the chosen of the Lord from tribulation and suffering. Throughout the history of

Israel, it is evident that those upon whom God's blessing and favor were bestowed endured the greatest contradiction and opposition. And among the favored, surely none were so greatly honored as the two who journeyed from Nazareth to Bethlehem in obedience to the summons from Rome. Behold Mary, the virgin of whom the prophet foretold—of David's royal line, the favored daughter! All generations shall call her blessed! And Joseph, her God-given spouse and protector—son of the house of David. How strange to find these two among the travelers who were making their way over the dusty roads! There was no singing nor rejoicing among them as in former times, when their forefathers had traveled these same roads on their way to Jerusalem to keep the holy feasts of the Lord. Now, all was heaviness and vexation of spirit.

Scripture has not recorded the incidents of that journey, nor has it drawn back the veil to reveal the thoughts and emotions of Joseph and Mary as they made the slow and perhaps painful journey toward their destination. Yet it may be the Holy Spirit will permit us a little glimpse into their hearts as we meditate upon them. For Joseph, it was an hour of great concern and responsibility. An unseemly time for journey! His tender devotion to Mary and her needs caused him to regret, if not resent, such a demand upon her. If ever she needed her home and its simple, familiar comforts it was at this hour. There, kind neighbors and friends would help to lighten her burden. From time to time his kind eyes searched her serene countenance, trying to detect a sign of her approaching ordeal. It is doubtful that many words passed between them... perhaps an occasional reassuring glance was exchanged, then they wrapped themselves again in their mantles of meditation. Joseph may have recalled the months of strange and seemingly unreal experiences through which he had passed since their betrothal: the dark hours of doubt and fear, the mingled wonder and joy, the shame and pain, which surrounded their marriage. Never was there a marriage like theirs since the world began! *How can it be,* he thought, *that this little one, this frail one, this meek one, riding along beside me, is about to give birth to the long-promised Deliverer and Redeemer of His people? Yet, had not Elizabeth said,* "Blessed art thou among women, and blessed is the fruit of thy womb"?

Now and then they stopped to rest the beasts. And it is likely that Joseph engaged in friendly conversation with their fellow-travelers. No doubt he listened to their talk of local events, in an effort to be courteous and kind. He heard their complaints about drouth and poor crops, and talk of hard times, and heavier taxes. Taxes! The word beat within his breast like the throb of a drum... taxes... taxes... taxes. Then, as they continued on their way, even the asses' feet kept time with it... taxes... taxes... taxes... This dread word called to his mind the centuries of oppression and slavery of his people under heathen kings. How strange it seemed to him that generation after generation they had been the prey of their enemies! His thoughts turned back to Babylon and to the long years of desolation and captivity. And, of course, to the Philistines!... those raiders and robbers! Nor could he forget the even darker period of bondage in the land of Egypt. Four hundred years of cruel labor and taxation under the lash of the Pharaohs! Israel had been reduced to abject slavery—mere chattel of the "underworld!" He thought, *That was their midnight hour, the hour just before their re-birth. How great had been the deliverance wrought by God through Moses! God had not forsaken His people! He had remembered His promise unto their forefathers and had raised up a deliverer to lead them out of the land of bondage. Great was His mercy and kindness! Had not Moses himself been spared from destruction in a miraculous way because his mother had not feared the wrath of the king?... His mother!... Jochebed... O favored woman! Her babe became the deliverer of his people. Her babe...* a quick glance at Mary's face... a flood of exultation! And again the words burned like fire within Joseph's breast: "*Fear not Joseph... son of David... take unto thee Mary... she shall bring forth a son... thou shalt call his name Jesus...*"

Mary, too, pondered many things in her heart as they journeyed. She scarcely noticed the barren hills and overcast skies. Everything around her seemed unreal, strange... detached. The voices of the travelers, the intermittent braying of the beasts, the tinkling of their bells—all blended into a discordant medley, an earthy undertone... Her heart sang again: "*My soul doth magnify the Lord... He that is mighty hath done to me great things...*" *Things I cannot understand*, she thought, "*but soon... very soon now... my eyes shall see my son, my little son... the Son of the Highest! Soon my own hands shall touch Him and dress Him; my arms shall hold Him to my breast. O my Lord... strength for this hour!* "Fear not, Mary, thou hast found favor with God." *Oh, I must not forget the angel's words; I must not be afraid. My time is near at hand—we must go on... on... to Bethlehem. O city of our father David! Did not the prophet say,* "And thou, Bethlehem, though thou be little... out of thee shall He come forth... to be ruler in Israel"? *Ruler in Israel! A king upon the throne of David? A king to whom we may pay glad homage and tribute? Tribute... tribute... tribute.* The word beat within her heart. And her ears seemed to catch the far-off echo of silver trumpets—the call to praise the Lord! *Then, shall His praise be made glorious as in the days of our father David. Then, shall He subdue all our enemies...* "He hath put down the mighty from their seat... He hath showed strength with His arm."

At last they reached the outskirts of Bethlehem. *It was near this very spot where Benjamin was born*, she thought. *It was here that Rachel breathed her last sigh as her babe was born. O mother in Israel, I honor thee! All mothers of Israel, I honor you; I, too, am about to become a mother in Israel. What was it Elizabeth had said?...* "The mother of my Lord..." *O God, how can it be?*

The Scripture has nothing more to say about the taxation of Joseph and Mary. But it does record a great deal about the hour of high tribute for which Mary had waited. We are all familiar with the story of that night of wonders, when Heaven bowed down and offered its shining glory to the little King. There was His star, transplendent among all the stars of the heavens, radiating its full praise! There were the angels, choiring through the skies their "Gloria In Excelsis Deo!" and bending to bless the earth with peace because He had descended to dwell with men! There were the shepherds who had seen His star and heard the angelic song, bringing the lowly adoration of mortals! Joseph and Mary were lost in wonder as they offered their own rich tribute of love and gratitude and worship unto the little Son of Heaven who lay at Mary's breast. And, later, when the wise men from the East came with costly gifts of gold, frankincense and myrrh, to worship the Babe, the joy of Joseph and Mary was complete. They had gone up to Bethlehem to enroll and pay taxes unto Caesar. They remained to fulfill the Word of God, and to pay their highest tribute to the King of Kings!

PART TWO

Centuries have passed into eternity since that wonderful night of our Savior's birth. And men are still paying taxes and tribute. Taxes... tribute! Thrones and kingdoms have been overthrown—new nations have been born; but, in spite of all our talk of democracy and liberty, we find ourselves living in a time of ever-increasing taxation. Like a tide it rises higher and higher, threatening the security of every nation. It is quite apparent that the "prince of this world" has sent out another decree that all the world should be taxed! All this is but an outward sign of the spiritual tax which is now being exacted from the children of God who, with the rest the world, suffer the oppression of the powers of darkness. How their cries ascend to heaven! Persecution, oppression, infirmities, distresses, vicissitudes, poverty, and the diabolical machinations of Satan—all these cruelly afflict the righteous. As it was with Job, no sooner does one calamity pass than another is at the door! They pray, they wrestle, they strive to rise above the tide—but little deliverance is wrought. Then, with Job, they ponder the mystery of the suffering of the elect; they taste of his despair and reproach, and finally come to an hour when they can say, "I know that my Redeemer liveth... when He hath tried me I shall come forth as gold." As gold—pure gold, refined in the fire heated seven-fold! "Ye have heard of the patience of Job, and have seen the end of the Lord; that the Lord is very pitiful, and of tender mercy." How rich and compensating was Job's latter end!

The Word of God reveals clearly that in the latter days the sufferings of the godly shall increase. The Apostle Peter, speaking expressly to those living at the end of the age, warns them to arm themselves to suffer. He reveals that it shall be a time of fiery trial—a time of heavy taxation! "Keep your foothold in the faith," he said, "and learn to pay the same *tax of suffering* as the rest of your brotherhood." (1 Peter 5:9, Moffatt) But he also reveals that it will be a time when the incorruptible inheritance of "great grace" and salvation will be brought into outward manifestation. "Wherefore, greatly rejoice... with joy unspeakable and full of glory: receiving the end of your faith..." And again he says, "Ye are a chosen generation, a royal priesthood... to show forth the *praises* of Him who hath called you out of darkness into His marvelous light." Over and over again he tells us to turn our tribulations into times of *tribute*—to praise and glorify God in the midst of the fires! The Apostle Paul speaks in a similar vein in his Epistles concerning the latter days, exhorting the faithful to render unto God full tribute of praise—rejoicing evermore. Are not these light afflictions working for us a far more exceeding and eternal weight of glory as we "look not at the things which are seen, but at the things which are not seen"?

Our every test, affliction and trial is an opportunity to glorify God and offer our hearty praise unto Him, to magnify and exalt His name. "Count it all joy..." How much joy we have missed by failing to reckon thus. What a blessed thing it is to give our money to the King; God loves a liberal giver! If this *tribute of praise* is not given, we shall most assuredly pay *taxes* to our Adversary—even to the last farthing! Doubts and fears, sighs and tears, complainings, murmurings, fault-findings, self-pity, jealousies—all these, and a variety of other negative thoughts and words and feelings which I need not enumerate, make up a rich tax for the coffers of Satan. How he feasts upon the bemoanings of the saints, growing fat on all their talk of his doings! How his power flourishes in the midst of the very church of the living God!

But there is a "faithful remnant" who has awakened to the meaning of this latter day, in whose hearts burns the hope of our Lord's glorious appearance and manifestation, culminating in His second advent. They fully realize they have been translated out of the kingdom of darkness into the kingdom of light, and that they owe no further tax to the prince of this world! *The coin of their hearts has been minted out of faith's pure gold, tried in the fire.* It bears the image and superscription of the King of Kings. They offer it freely unto Him with songs of praise, shouts of victory, and rejoice with great joy that they are privileged to suffer with Him. These will not have to share the lot of "murmuring Israel" who, throughout the ages, were delivered again and again into the hands of their enemies because they failed to give God full tribute of service and praise. (Reference Deuteronomy 28:47,48.)

In this remnant there are found those who, like Zacharias (meaning Jehovah remembers), experience times of heavenly visitation while "burning incense and praying in the temple of the Lord." They, too, are sometimes stricken dumb because they doubt that which is told them. But after weeks of silence and waiting, their mouths are opened again to prophesy when they behold "signs" and "forerunners" of His appearing. They glory in the light of the Dayspring from on high, and rejoice in His redemption.

And there are those, like the beloved Elizabeth (oath of God), who have known long years of barrenness while others were flourishing and fruitful. Reproach and disappointment have been their lot, notwithstanding their prayers and devotion. Then, unexpectedly, there comes a heavenly visitation! "Sing, O barren, thou that didst not bear; break forth into singing, and cry aloud..." There is a quickening, a leaping within, and a mighty infilling of the Holy Ghost. And the word—a song of wonder springs from their lips!

Faithful hearts like Anna (grace), have been daily performing their vows of prayer. How blest are these "widows" of the Lord, who know full well that soon their eyes shall behold their God in the flesh! They are voicing their praise!

And the Simeons (to hear), the sons of Jacob, who have ears to hear the Word from above, are watching with faith and worship. They are "just men and devout," waiting for the consolation of Israel; and the Holy Ghost is upon them. They are fully assured that they shall see His great Salvation.

Likewise, from among the sons of men, the Holy Spirit has sought out those whose hearts are like Joseph's. Men of fervent and tender spirit, devoted unto the will of God. They have followed His call, even though it led them "without the camp," bearing reproach and the misunderstanding of their brethren. These have paid a *heavy tax of suffering*! But they are reckoning it *joy* as they make their way toward the shining hour of His latter day manifestation in His many-membered Body.

What of the Marys? Giving all honor unto the little Maid of Nazareth, whom God has uniquely favored among women of all generations, may we dare to say that in this latter day our Father has been seeking for Mary-hearts? Yes, we joyfully proclaim it! And among women, He has found those who are eager to give themselves unto Him with devotion similar to that which she displayed. They can find no more fitting words than Mary's with which to voice their dedication: "Behold the handmaid of the Lord; be it unto me according to Thy word." *Upon these is levied a cruel tax of shame, reproach, contradiction and anguish.* Their way, too, becomes one of separation and deprivation as they journey toward His appointed Hour! *Taxes or tribute?* They regard not the price of their submission unto God. They are lost in the wonder of His indwelling presence, and in the living hope of His approaching manifestation among men. As they journey, their hearts are lifted in adoration, and their voices soar above earth's din in an exultant Magnificat! They have become God's living, embodied Praise on earth. "Blessed is she that hath believed: for there shall be a performance of those things which were told her of the Lord."

THE LAMB OF GOD
(AT THE FOOT OF THE CROSS)

Frances Metcalfe

Behold the Lamb of God that taketh away the sins of the world!

"Wherefore, gird up the loins of your mind, be sober, and *hope* to the *end* for the *grace* that is to be brought unto you at the *revelation* of *Jesus Christ*; as obedient children, not fashioning yourselves according to the former lusts in your ignorance; but as He which hath called you is holy, so be ye holy in all manner of conversation (behavior); because it is written; 'Be ye holy for I am holy.' And if ye call on the Father, who without respect of persons judgeth according to every man's work, pass the time of your sojourning here in fear; for as much as ye know that ye were not redeemed with corruptible things as silver and gold, from your vain conversation (habits of life) received by tradition from your fathers: but with *the precious blood of Christ*, as of a Lamb *without blemish* and *without spot*; who verily was foreordained before the foundation of the world, but was manifest in these last times for you, who by Him do believe in God, that *raised Him up from the dead*, and *gave Him glory*, that your faith and hope might be in God!" (1 Peter 1:13-21)

Written to those "Who are kept by the *power of God*, through *faith*, unto *salvation* ready to be revealed at the *last time* (to be unveiled at the end of the age—Weymouth.)" (1 Pet. 1:5)

The writings of this booklet were given by the inspiration of the Holy Spirit. "The testimony of Jesus is the spirit of prophecy." (Revelation 19:10)

PREFACE

As you read these pages, please remember that most were written decades ago. What they contain, however, is as true today as it was then. And perhaps even more necessary, because we are seeing an increase in miracles and signs and wonders, the "greater works" promised for these last days.

Our God must have prepared vessels, and part of that preparation comes as we meet the increase in the attacks of our enemy, and let HIM be victorious in us. "Be sober, be vigilant; because your adversary the devil, as a roaring lion, walketh about, seeking whom he may devour: whom resist steadfast in the faith, knowing that the same afflictions are accomplished in your brethren that are in the world." (1 Pet. 5:8-9)

We are aware that the message of the Cross, of dying to self and all that we desire for our personal gratification, is not a popular subject. But St. Paul considered it vital, and could say, "I am crucified with Christ; nevertheless I live; yet not I, but Christ liveth in me..." (Gal. 2:20) O that this may be true in each of our lives—that HE may be glorified.

—Marian Joy Pickard

Jesus is Alive, He's alive forevermore
Jesus is Alive and is standing at the door.
Soon He shall appear—
His hour is very near!
Jesus is ALIVE!

—M.P.

AT THE FOOT OF THE CROSS

At the foot of the Cross
They stood—
The mourners and the mockers—
His friends and His foes—
His lovers and His despisers;
Gazing upon that dreadful sight—
The excruciate agony of the Divine Victim—
The Lamb of God.
They gazed—
And some mocked, and some derided;
Some believed—while others cursed—
But one, from whom His Body,
In condescension He had assumed—
Leaned upon the breast of another
Grief-panged lover.
These two,
And a FEW
Gazed, and knew
The inmost martyrdom
Of a broken, bleeding heart,
As they offered themselves
With HIM, to the Father
An eternal holocaust!

So, at the foot of the Cross
They stood, and gazed—
But Heaven could not gaze
Upon a sight so horrible,
For Heaven saw
That which the earth could not see—

Saw the Eternal Father
Lay upon the Everlasting SON—
THE SINS OF THE WORLD!
Saw the SON become SIN!
Saw the Father heap upon Him
The terror of Divine wrath
And indignation!

At this awesome sight, the Holy Angels
Fell upon their faces—AGHAST!
And death-like silence
Settled like a mantle upon Heaven.

And at that dreadful moment
When the Father turned away His face—
Heaven's portals rolled together and closed—
Closed in the face (the pain-marred face)
Of One whose eyes had ever been fixed
In undying love, upon the FATHER.
What else could the sun do, but veil ITS face—
Even the earth itself, exceedingly quaked
And reeled upon its axis!
And the powers of darkness reigned supreme
On earth, as in Hell! This was their "hour"
As HE had foretold—
Darkest, maddest hour of all time!

Centuries have rolled away—and yet today
The world still stands at the foot of the Cross
And gazes at the sight
Angels could not bear to see.
And still there are the mourners and

Mockers—His friends and His foes—
His lovers and His despisers.
Some still mock and curse,
Others are indifferent,
But a FEW, as of old, BELIEVE—
Falling at His feet in ardent Love,
Pray, that they, with Him,
May drink the bitter cup—
And know the excruciate bliss
Of a broken, bleeding heart,
As they offer themselves, WITH HIM,
Unto the Father—an eternal Holocaust!

—F.M.

"Now before the feast of the Passover, when Jesus knew that His hour was come that He should depart out of this world unto the Father, having loved His own which were in the world, He loved them unto the end." (John 13:1)

HE OPENED NOT HIS MOUTH

Every word proceeding out of the mouth of our Lord was charged with the *dunamis* of God—it was quick and powerful and sharper than any two-edged sword, yet He won His greatest battle on earth by a weapon even more potent—a sublime, majestic silence!

"He was oppressed and He was afflicted yet He opened not His mouth; He is brought as a lamb [sheep] to the slaughter, and as a sheep before her shearers is dumb, so He openeth not His mouth." (Isaiah 53:7)

He had spoken deep and wonderful things to His disciples. He had taken them apart alone, to give them His final instructions and teachings. Grace and Truth had poured from His lips like a fountain of Life. His heart had burned within Him as He told them the deep mysteries of the Kingdom and the eternal purposes of the Father. And they, His nearest, dearest ones were bewildered and fearful. They had listened with questioning minds and dull hearts, unable to grasp the import of His words. How He yearned to tell them ALL, to declare unto them the whole counsel of God, but He could only say, "Ye cannot bear it now." And then the hour came when strange words fell from His lips, words which stirred them to dark forebodings.

"Hereafter I will not talk much with you, for the prince of this world cometh and [he] hath nothing in Me." (John 14:30)

So, to every disciple of the Cross, if we follow all the way to Calvary, there comes an hour when our lips, too, must keep silence—when words utterly fail—when there is no answering back. We, too, may hear words similar to those spoken long ago to Him: "Answerest Thou nothing? What is it which these witness against Thee?" (Mark 14:60)

And in that hour, if we have the Lamb nature of God, we shall, indeed we *must,* "hold our peace." (Matt. 26:62-63) "Therefore, the prudent shall keep silence in that time; for it is an evil time." (Amos 5:13)

"I'll go with Him through the Garden...
"I'll go with Him, with Him, all the way."

Our lips have often sung this, but few of us remembered that it was in the Garden, in the trysting place of prayer for Christ and His dear ones, where He met cruel betrayal at the hands of one He loved.

Only three, His most privileged Disciples, had gone with Him to pray. And even these had slumbered through His most crucial hour—an hour when He had resisted evil until Blood came from

His pores—yet no harsh word came from His lips to them. His disappointment in them was great, but His reproof was kind. How we marvel, and weep, when we comprehend, even in a small measure the Grace of our Lord manifest toward His followers—displayed even in the hours of intense agony! "Having loved His own, He loved them *to the end.*" He loved them in spite of their selfishness, pride, lack of faith, and their neglect. He loved them in spite of their human weaknesses and failures. Of them it is written: "They all forsook Him and fled." (Mk. 14:50) But, of Him, "He loved them to the end." (Jn. 13:1) Let us rejoice and give thanks that today, as in that dark hour, having loved us, His own, He loves us to the end!

If we are taking the way of the Cross, we must not be too surprised when we come face to face with a Judas. Are we prepared to meet this crisis of treachery and betrayal with the meek and patient spirit of the Son of God? Shall we be able to look into the eyes of such a one and in all sincerity say, "Friend, why art thou come?" (Matt. 26:50) The Spirit answers: "There are very few who can follow their Lord through betrayal, accusation and judgment in this manner." Nothing is more bitter to our souls than falsity, hypocrisy and treachery. Yet it was written, for this very day: "Ye shall be betrayed both by parents and brethren and kinsfolk and friends and some of you shall they cause to be put to death." (Lk. 21:16) And, "A man's foes are they of his own household." (Matt. 10:36)

David, in his day, tasted such a bitter cup: "For it was not an enemy that reproached me, then could I have borne it; neither was it he that hated me that did magnify himself against me; then I would have hid myself from him: but it was thou, a man my equal... mine acquaintance. We took sweet counsel together and walked into the house of God in company." (Psalm 55:12-14)

It is inevitable that our enemy should be found in the very inner circle of our heart, from our natural or spiritual family, for only those whom we love deeply and who know us well, can sell us into the hands of our religious enemies. It is from their hands we take the cup, bitter with jealousy, ambition and avarice; it is from their lips we receive the sickening kiss of death. Who among us is able for *these* things? Has the Son of God so possessed us that in that hour we can call them, "friend"? Can we say, with our Lord, and with the early saints: "Lay not this sin to their charge"? (Acts 7:60) Can we "hold our peace" and enter that sublime silence?

Heaven and earth witnesses the trial of our soul. Mere human strength cannot sustain us. But nothing is more detestable in the eyes of God, and man, than a traitor. An honest, open enemy we may respect, but the deceitful, cowardly traitor arouses the fighting blood of any godly heart. Equally bitter is the persecution into which we are betrayed, for we receive it from the hands of the religious leaders of the day. It was the religious leaders who were our Lord's most bitter enemies. And, in every age, His followers have met a death struggle with those who have stopped short somewhere along the road to Calvary. "Jealousy is cruel as the grave. The coals thereof are coals of fire, which hath a most vehement flame." (Song of Solomon 8:6) It has kindled the pyres of the martyrs and still flames on, ravaging, devouring and devastating.

It has been said that every soul is a potential John or a potential Judas. However true this may be, a noted saint of the early centuries is reported to have said: "I labor for every soul as though he were to become the most Christlike soul on earth, yet I labor wisely and with discretion for I know that that soul may become the sharpest tool of Satan for my destruction." It is reported of Madame Guyon that often when she was suffering and laboring with a soul, the Holy Spirit would reveal to her that later on that one would turn on her and rend her, bringing reproach upon her. For all of this she labored lovingly for that one, manifesting perfect love and sacrifice as unto the Lord. Contrast her Lamb-like spirit with the spirit we find among many of the Lord's people today. Even among the so-called "deeper saints" the usual reaction to accusation and persecution is one of indignation and a strong effort to clear one's name, even with strife and anger, if necessary. A spirit of vindication seems to possess them, and at any cost their reputation and position must be maintained! Do they enter into the sublime silence of The Lamb of God? No, they are more apt to devote the remainder of their lives to the task of contradicting and offsetting the attack of the enemy.

A few, it is true, will take a way of milder resistance. Yet, they will allow inward bitterness and suspicion to poison their hearts and undermine their souls. Others become provoked or discouraged and give up the battle altogether, doubting their former experiences and the leadings of the Holy Spirit. O blind and foolish disciples! It is our glory to follow our Lord through the Garden! It is our glory and unspeakable privilege to drink of His cup, to receive the Judas kiss, to be brought to false judgment and to seem to fail completely.

Can we escape this way of the Cross? Certainly! There are many ways to sell out cheaply to betray our Lord. We can compromise and back down—take the popular way of men-pleasers—use our gifts and personalities to attract people to ourselves—become influential and successful. Yes, in every one of us is a potential Judas, and men may never know that we have betrayed our Lord. They may even commend us for being sensible and less extreme, less intense. But for those who have looked full into HIS face, and have drunk from the passion of His Divine Heart, there is no thought of escape. He has kindled a Divine Flame within our frail hearts—a supernatural desire to suffer with Him, to bear His Cross, to partake of His agony vicariously. And we, following on, go with Him through the Garden of Gethsemane and enter into that "sublime silence." We shall learn wonderful and terrible things in that silence, *providing we are kept in perfect peace!* Break not this Divine silence! More battles are lost at this point than any other. Divine grace shall sustain you, and lovingly, meekly, you too shall be led as a sheep to the slaughter, to the grave, to Paradise, to the glorious and eternal resurrection and triumph! This is the mystery of the Cross of Jesus Christ, my Lord.

> I am walking today on the Blood-sprinkled way
> The way that my Savior trod;
> My heart and my eyes are now fixed on the prize
> That awaits at the Throne of God;
> This Blood-sprinkled way is the blessed old way
> The martyrs and saints journeyed down,
> O, I'm glad I can say I'm on the Blood-sprinkled way
> The Way of the Cross and the Crown.
>
> —Frances Metcalfe

THE SECRET OF THE CROSS

> One day His Voice smiled into my ear:
>   "Carry thy cross, child, and have no fear;
> Let none see thee to sympathize;
>   Let me wipe those tears from out your eyes.
> Carry it hidden—covered with beauty—
>   Not in self-pity, nor in grim duty;
> But so glorified, that none can guess
>   There's a cross beneath such loveliness!"
>
> "Carry it gladly, with a smile—
>   Don't come sadly, even a mile;
> Cover it well, yes, with flower-sheath—
>   None will guess what is underneath.

God, alone, must see and know
      Thy bleeding heart—He wants it so!
"This is thy cross, then," He said to me,
      "To suffer, thus, when men can't see."

"No cross you bear, when all can see—
      And sympathize, and weep with thee;
Misunderstood—mine are—" He saith,
      "As even was I, in life and death.
Take the way of the cross, with joy and song,
      Suffering loss—suffering wrong—
Covering woe and sorrow with blossoms fair,
      That none may know the cross you bear."

"Let men see only the flowers abloom
      And be lifted by their sweet perfume—
Sweet fragrance floating everywhere,
      Reminiscent of joyful praise and prayer."
O, teach me, Lord, to bear like Thee—
      In the great grace of Calvary—
My cross, disguised in roses sweet—
      All unsurmised by those I meet!

              —N.L.

JESUS—SWEET LITTLE LAMB

Sweet little Lamb of Mary,
      The fairest of all the flock;
How pure and soft is thy woolly fleece,
      Dear little Lamb without spot!
Sweet little Lamb of Mary,
      Held close in her gentle arms—
Her mother-heart yearns within her,
      To shield Thee from dangers and harms.

Sweet little Lamb of Mary,
      Cuddled in her loving breast,
Why does she weep those bitter tears,
      Why is her spirit oppressed?
Sweet little Lamb of Mary,
      Why does she tremble and sigh—
Does she know of the pain that awaits Thee—
      Has she glimpsed the death Thou wilt die?

Sweet little Lamb of Mary,
      Thou art the LAMB of GOD,
Born to be slain, a sacrifice,
      Born to pour out Thy Blood;
Sweet little Lamb of Mary,
      Unspeakable Gift of God,
The sins of the world are washed away
      In Thy Holy Crimson Flood.

Sweet little Lamb of Mary,
      From the world's foundation slain,

Thou who wert dead—art RISEN—
    And behold, Thou art living again!
Sweet little Lamb of Mary,
    Thy triumph, the Father reveals—
For Thou hast PREVAILED and art worthy
    To open the Book and the SEALS!

—F.M.

HIS CROSS AND MINE

It Was His Cross:
>   The bitter gall to drink
>   Was for the Son of Heaven;
>   Not His—from pain to shrink—
>   His soul the vow had given.

>   For vesture holy cast they lots—
>   (Scene meet for angel tears)
>   Remembrance of His agony
>   To last their guilty years!

This Is My Cross:
>   The gall, sweet-tasting now,
>   Heaven's nectar in its sting;
>   And oil for nail-pierced hand
>   Will Christ, the Healer bring!

>   Christ is my Righteous Robe
>   To clothe my unrobed shame;
>   Their rabble voices, hush, My Lord,
>   Their obscene words disclaim!

>   His was the fevered brow,
>   Mine—cooled by His sweet breath;
>   Can I then, greatly fear
>   Though dark and deep—my death?

—C.V.

"Worthy is the LAMB that was SLAIN, to receive power, and riches, and wisdom, and strength, and honor, and glory, and blessing. And every creature which is in heaven, and on the earth and under the earth, and such as are in the sea, and all that are in them, heard I saying; 'Blessing, and honor, and glory, and power, be unto Him that sitteth upon the throne, and unto the LAMB for ever and ever.'" (Revelation 5:12-13)

THE CROSS AND THE CUP

Frances Metcalfe

THE CROSS AND THE CUP

Thy blood, O Lord, is my drink divine,
Offered by Thine own hands to me,
A chalice brimming with crimson wine,
Flowing from Calvary.

Thy cup was drained in Gethsemane,
Mingled with bitter tears and blood.
Oh let me drink of it now with Thee,
Jesus, my Lord and God!

"As oft as ye shall receive this cup,
Do it," Thou saidst, "Remembering Me;
Proclaim My death as ye lift it up—
Forget not Mine agony."

The cup once bitter is now made sweet;
Death swallowed up in Life, I see,
And kneeling low at Thy nail-scarred feet,
I taste immortality!

I take the Cup of Salvation,
Filled with the Lamb's precious blood;
I drink everlasting Life,
The life of the Son of God!

Are ye able to drink of the cup that I shall drink of, and to be baptized with the baptism that I am baptized with?' They say unto Him, 'We are able.' And He saith unto them, 'Ye shall drink indeed of My cup, and be baptized with the baptism that I am baptized with...'" (Matthew 20:22-23)

"Lo, winter is past, the rain is over and gone; the flowers appear on the earth!" Passover-time... Resurrection-time... Such is the season of passion and pain and sorrow; of hope and joy and rejoicing—the most sacred and significant season of the year! Death and life beckon us, speak to us, anew; and nature reenacts the glorious drama of rebirth after seeming oblivion. It is a time for the renewing of "first love" and of the vows it inspires... an "acceptable day"... a time of beginning again.

"This month shall be unto you the beginning of months: it shall be the first month of the year to you." So spoke the Lord unto Moses and Aaron in the land of Egypt. And from that day all Israel kept Jehovah's sacred New Year in the month of Abib. When, at the time of the vernal equinox, the new moon appeared in the western sky, it announced the month of beginnings to Israel. The First Passover-time ushered in a *new day*, opened up a *new way*, and promised them a *new land* for their possession. It meant deliverance, liberty, and the manifest presence of God in the midst of His people!

Israel observed the first Passover with obedience and godly fear. The season did not begin with rejoicing and feasting, but with repentance, sacrifice, and the threat of a reign of death. Leaven—a type of sin—was to be searched out and taken away from every dwelling place in the camp, in preparation for "the feast of unleavened bread." An unblemished male lamb was to be provided for every family and sacrificed on Passover Eve—that dread fourteenth day of Abib when the Angel of Death was to slay Egypt's firstborn. So impressive and wonderful were the events of this first Passover, as recorded in Exodus 12, that even today, centuries later, the Orthodox Jew still keeps Passover in a type. And all Christians understand that this Egyptian Passover prefigured the greater ecumenical Passover which was fulfilled at Calvary by the offering of the Lamb of God. (Matt. 26-27)

"Christ our Passover is sacrificed for us. Therefore let us keep the feast, not with old leaven, neither with the leaven of malice and wickedness; but with the unleavened bread of sincerity and truth." (1 Corinthians 5:7-8)

Even as Jesus was "the Lamb slain from the foundation of the world," so there is a certain sense in which *this sacrifice is perpetuated from age to age in those members of Christ's mystical body who are able to partake of His passion and death.* The Holy Spirit has a way of focalizing and personalizing the truth. The sons of God, by the power of the Spirit, are given to partake of the experiences and passion of the First-begotten—according to their capacity and desire to do so.

St. Paul *thirsted* for such a union with Christ as would permit him to "know Him in the power of His resurrection, and the fellowship of His suffering, being made conformable unto His death." And we have good reason to believe that he did indeed enter into such a communion. He spoke frequently of being crucified with Christ, buried with Him, *planted* in His death; and of being raised again in resurrection power. Once he said: "But we had the sentence of death in ourselves, that we should not trust in ourselves, but in God which raiseth the dead." He experienced a daily death, not unto sin—for he had long since dealt with the sin question—but in participation with the sufferings of Christ. Again and again he was delivered over to the forces of death. "So then *death* worketh in *us*, but *life* in *you*," he cried. He knew—as all consecrated saints have known—that life springs forth out of death, strength out of weakness, victory out of seeming defeat.

To Paul, these "dyings" were very real. They were far more than a mere "reckoning." He was beaten with many stripes, shipwrecked, stoned, starved and abandoned. Again and again he was tempted to despair of life. Because Paul so fully participated in the fellowship of Christ's sufferings, he experienced a commensurate enduement of resurrection life. When he cried out, "I can do all things through Christ which strengtheneth me," he meant literally *all things!* For him it was a practical reality, stated in a letter written from *prison* after at least twelve years of superhuman *toil, privation* and *ill-usage.* The one who could confidently say, "My God shall supply all your needs according to His riches in glory by Christ Jesus," knew about poverty, hunger, physical pain and weakness from first-hand experience, and had learned how to "take pleasure in necessities" and to "glory in tribulation." He was "in journeyings often, in perils of waters, in perils of robbers, in perils by mine own countrymen, in perils by the heathen, in perils in the city, in perils in the wilderness, in perils in the sea, in perils among false brethren; in *weariness* and *painfulness*, in watchings often, in *hunger* and *thirst*; in fastings often, in *cold* and *nakedness*." (2 Cor. 11:26-27)

Our own experiences seem rather pale in comparison with those of Paul's and of other apostolic saints. I am reminded of a line from a poem which speaks of "Our *little* journeys into death, our *little* risings from the tomb."

"It is a faithful saying: for *if* we be *dead* with Him we shall also *live* with Him; *if* we *suffer*, we shall also reign with Him." Gradually our capacity for His love and suffering and heart-travail increases, and as it does we bear more and more fruit which shall redound to the glory of God. Not *too* many in the earth are thirsting to share His sufferings, to bear His cross, to drink His cup. "Are ye able to drink of the cup that I shall drink of, and to be baptized with the baptism that I am baptized with?" He asked His disciples of old. And, as a song has well phrased it, "The sturdy dreamers answered, 'To the death we follow Thee.'" But when the hour came they found His cup too bitter, His baptism too fiery. "They all forsook Him and fled." They were not able at that time to enter into His sufferings and death. However, it brings great joy to our hearts to know that there came a day for each of them when they, by the grace of God, were well able to do so as, one by one, they too laid down their lives for the Gospel.

"Christ is our Passover Lamb!" Let us partake of His chalice without fear. As we drink of it we shall find a strange transmutation taking place. The bitter will become sweet. It has the *savor* of death, but the *essence* of life. As we drain it to the dregs it will become the very nuptial cup of the heavenly Bridegroom with which He and His bride pledge their vows. O brimming up! O ruby-red wine of eternal life and love! "Drink, yea, drink abundantly, O Beloved!" Resurrection power is in the cup!

PSALMS OF THE KING FOR THE LATTER DAY

Frances Metcalfe

INTRODUCTION

THE PSALMS—THE PRAISES OF THE LORD

The book of Psalms is termed in Hebrew, Sepher Tehillim, which scholars claim is derived from hal or halal, meaning: to praise, to move briskly, to irradiate, shine or translate. It may well be called "the book of shinings forth, irradiations, manifestations or displays of divine wisdom and love, exhibited in God's dealings with men." In them Christ and His Church and coming Kingdom are prefigured. In them is found prophecy of the highest order. Yet their greatest beauty and significance lie in the worship and praise they embody. So their most familiar title is "The Praises of Israel" or "The Praises of the Lord."

"All the music of the human heart is in the Psalms," said Gladstone, "and these perhaps had more to do with shaping the national character of Israel than had all its kings and priests. If David had written a doctrinal treatise, instead of the Psalms, his name might never have come down to us. Judaism might not have survived its birth period if it had not been a *singing* religion. More than any other class, the prophets of Israel and Judah embodied and preserved the national faith. *Prophecy* and *music* were indissolubly wedded. The schools of the prophets were schools of music. Sacred song and sacrifice continued to be the mediums of Jewish worship as long as the temple stood. And Christianity was born to the strains of celestial anthems."

Not only was the Christian Church born in song, but it has been *preserved* and *revived* from century to century by the songs of the Spirit. It too finds its highest worship in the sacred song. The singing of Psalms, hymns and spiritual songs is an evidence of being filled with the Spirit and of "letting the Word of Christ dwell in you richly." (Eph. 5:19; Col. 3:16)

The famed Dr. Donne said: "The Psalms are the manna of the Church. Some are imperial Psalms, commanding all affection and spreading themselves over all occasions—catholic, universal Psalms, that apply themselves to all necessities. David hath dressed out religion in such a rich and beautiful garment of divine poesy, as beseemeth her majesty, in which being arrayed she can stand up before the eyes, even of her enemies, in more royal state, than any personification of love, or glory or pleasure to which highly gifted mortals have devoted their genius."

"The Hebrew Psalter is the most ancient collection of poems in the world," says Adam Clarke, "it was composed long before those in which ancient Greece and Rome have gloried. Our blessed Lord used the book of Psalms and quoted from it. This stamps it with the highest authority. And that He and His disciples used it as a book of devotion, we learn from their singing the Hallel at His last supper, which we know was composed of Psalms 113-118. The Psalms were used by the Christian Church from the earliest times, especially in praising God."

To quote F.B. Meyer: "The Psalm really began with David. Its lyric beauty and tender grace; its rhythmic measure; its exuberant hallelujahs and plaintive lamentations; its inimitable expression of the changeful play of light and shade over the soul; its blending of nature and godliness; its references to the life of men and the world, as regarded from the standpoint of God—these elements in the Psalter which have endeared it to holy souls in every age owe their origin to the poetic, heaven-touched soul of the sweet singer of Israel."

It was David who composed the majority of the Psalms. It was he who utilized them so gloriously in the worship of the Lord. It is to him that we are indebted for a concept of praise and worship never before revealed on earth. It has been said that he heard the songs of the angels and transposed them into mortal language. The Psalms are more widely read and loved than any other portion of the Bible. The Psalms have inspired countless sermons and songs throughout the three thousand years since they first were sung. Rich in prophecy and revelation, they speak eloquently to us in this latter day. And the same Holy Spirit that moved upon the fervent heart of David now creates in our hearts songs of praise and prophecy. How blessed, how glorious is this Davidic way of worship!

"The Psalms are a mirror in which each man sees the motions of his own soul. They express in exquisite words the kinship which every thoughtful human heart craves to find with the supreme, unchanging, loving God, who will be to him a protector, guardian and friend. They utter the ordinary experiences, the familiar thoughts of men; but they give to these a width of range, an intensity, a depth, and an elevation, which transcend the capacity of the most gifted. They translate into speech the spiritual passion of the loftiest genius; they also utter, with the beauty born of truth and simplicity, and with exact agreement between the feeling and the expression, the inarticulate and humble longings of the unlettered peasant. So it is that, in every country, the language of the Psalms has become part of the daily life of nations, passing into their proverbs and literature, mingling with their conversation, and used at every critical stage of existence."

—Rowland E. Prothero

THE PSALM OF THE MESSIAH-KING

The second Psalm is a remarkable prophetic song of the King and His Kingdom. It is supposed that David composed this after he had taken Jerusalem from the Jebusites and made it the head of the Kingdom. Surely no one else was ever given such inspired visions of the Kingdom. For David not only dreamed of it, but actually lived out much of its reality in a typical manner. This song reflected his own bitter experiences as he suffered and warred for the throne. It was forged in the intense fires of his own suffering, and sprang forth, for all the world to hear, after his hour of triumph. No wonder it strikes fire in men's breasts century after century!

The Apostles quoted freely from this Psalm in their day. (See Acts 4:24-31; 13:16-23.) This Psalm has inspired countless songs and sermons during the Church age. And, in the latter day, the Holy Spirit has frequently impressed it upon the hearts of those who are being prepared for the Endtime harvest and the birth of the Kingdom on earth. Every verse of this Psalm has been highlighted to us during the years of our preparation. Here is a song for us to memorize, sing and assimilate. Its greater fulfillment has already begun!

Spurgeon comments on this Psalm as follows: "The establishment of David upon his throne, notwithstanding the opposition of his enemies, is the subject of this Psalm. David sustains in it a two-fold character, literal and allegorical. If we read over the Psalm, first with an eye to the literal David, the meaning is obvious, and put beyond all dispute by sacred history. If we take another survey of the

Psalm as relative to the spiritual David, Jesus Christ, a noble series of events immediately rises to view, and the meaning becomes more evident, as well as more exalted. New light is continually being cast upon its phraseology, and fresh weight and dignity are added to the sentiments."

The way to the throne proved to be a stormy and tragic pathway for David. When Samuel's presence in Jesse's house had brought an astonishing summons to David, he was living a peaceful, worshipful life with his father's sheep. It is likely that he would have continued this pastoral life if his appointment to the Kingdom had not changed his course. At first this change was not evident. After his anointing he returned again to his sheep. There was no sudden outward move toward the power and glory of the throne. The one great difference in David can be stated in a few simple words, "The Spirit of the Lord came upon David from that day forward." The Spirit of God! How revolutionary is His power! From that day forward David moved on toward his full entry into the Kingdom, and his pathway became increasingly hazardous.

Here is the pattern for each of us to whom the call of the Kingdom has come. We too were once peacefully settled with the flock of our Lord. How dearly we loved the church of our choice! How established and comfortable we felt, serving Him in various ways, looking forward to His second coming—expecting it to overtake us while we moved among the flock. Then, suddenly, surprisingly, there came a call to the Kingdom! Kingdom light shone upon our pathway! A Kingdom messenger was sent to us—seen or unseen—and a new anointing was poured out upon us. We heard unbelievable words. Our hearts were stirred and enfired by visions of the glories of the Kingdom of God on earth. How often has this pattern been repeated!

Sooner or later the Kingdom vision is sure to be given to those who are faithfully following the Great Shepherd, obeying His words "seek ye first the Kingdom of God and His righteousness." He who has been known as our Savior and Shepherd becomes manifest to us as our King! The King of Glory, the Messiah-King! How wonderful is this vision of glory to come! We become intensely aware of His desire to reign on earth as in heaven. We begin to realize that it is the Gospel of the *Kingdom* that is going to be preached to all creatures before the end can come. We see the Church-age gradually fading from view, merging into the manifest power and glory of the Kingdom! We learn with amazement that we too are called to share that glory and to reign with Christ in Kingdom power. It is overwhelming!

Yet, like David, we are sure to find that the way into the Kingdom is long and tortuous. We do not at once leave the sheep and proceed to the throne. No, we go quietly back to the flock for a time, just as he did, and begin the long preparation for our new entrance into the Kingdom. We find that to be *born* into the Kingdom is a matter of grace; but to *enter* into it as a mature son, destined to reign with Christ and receive the rewards of the Kingdom, requires much discipline, faith, suffering, warfare and sacrifice.

The New Testament teachings confirm all that David learned so painstakingly. "The Kingdom of heaven suffereth violence, and the violent take it by force." "We must *by much tribulation* enter the Kingdom of heaven." In the first chapter of 2 Peter, we are shown the requirements for an abundant entrance into the Kingdom. And Paul too had much to say about the training for the Kingdom. Jesus, of course, gave us complete instructions for the Kingdom and summed them all up in two main figures—the *child* and the *servant of all.* He said that it is to the "little flock" that the Father will give the Kingdom. The Second Psalm speaks eloquently to that little flock. And if you are found among them, rejoice! Yes, they are, as Amos said, "the flock of the slaughter." But, praise God! they know that "the saints of God shall take the Kingdom and possess it forevermore." (See Daniel 7:18)

Today as never before, the heathen—the nations—are raging, the people are imagining vain things, and the rulers of the earth are set against the Lord and His anointed. In David's day it was only a handful, by comparison, who opposed the Lord. Communism has risen like a great dark flood—covering much of the earth. One of its tenets is that "after having deposed all present world rulers, we shall ascend into heaven and force God Himself from His throne." Hatred against God and Christ has never risen to a higher peak! And all over the world countless lambs of God have been led to the slaughter! David, who suffered the pangs of hell for the sake of the Kingdom, would scorn the modernist church that still dreams of the Kingdom of God coming peacefully and gradually without any outward strife. The derision and wrath of the Father is even now being manifest on earth.

Of a truth the Father has set His King upon His holy hill Zion, "Out of Zion shall go forth the law." God has a real Zion on earth—a Kingdom people, in whose hearts He is already enthroned. The King is great in Zion! He is honored and feared and loved and served! And by the power of the Holy Spirit He does reign through these people, to a great extent, even now. He shines out through them, revealing His glory to those whose eyes are opened to see. He speaks through them to those who have anointed ears. Blessed Zion! The King is in her midst and the Highest Himself shall establish her!

"Thou art My son, this day have I begotten thee." This Word is quoted in the New Testament as pertaining to the resurrection of Christ. (Acts 13:33) It is also quoted in the book of Hebrews. There comes a time in our own lives too when the Holy Spirit witnesses with our spirit—and we hear these words deep in our heart: "Thou art My son, this day have I begotten thee." We are begotten in Christ, unto eternal sonship. What wonder! What glory!

169

"Ask of me, and I shall give thee the heathen (nations) for thine inheritance and the uttermost parts of the earth for thy possession." How often has the Spirit impressed this verse upon those who are hidden away in intercession. My heart leaps again as it did when I first heard it. I began then to intercede for all the nations of the earth. Such a prayer call! We learn by this Word that although we are called to reign as kings, we are to begin our ministry by praying as priests! "A royal order of Kings and Priests" indeed! But the priestly work must be done first. David spent many years in worship and prayer, after his anointing, before his open manifestation began. Jesus, although He did announce His Kingdom at His first coming, did not come to the throne at that time. He has been engaged in intercession for two thousand years. We do not hasten to Kingdom glory. There is much first to be wrought in prayer and praise.

As we read on we find the promise of ruling with a rod of iron, and of shattering all evil. This too is given directly to us. Jesus, Himself, confirms it in His appearing to John. "And he that overcometh, and keepeth My works unto the end, to him shall I give power over the nations; and he shall rule them with a rod of iron; as the vessels of a potter shall they be broken to shivers: even as I received of My Father." (Rev. 2:26-28) Then He adds a glorious promise, "And I will give him THE MORNING STAR."

The closing portion of the Psalm is spoken to earthly rulers. But in a sense we too in Christ are rulers and judges in Israel—as the Spirit moves in us. This Word, in any case, has been often quickened to us. "Serve the Lord with fear, rejoice with trembling. Kiss the Son!" Yes, by the inspiration of the Holy Spirit, we have been taught to have a godly fear—an awe of the Most High—which saves us from presumption and false security. The place in the Throne is most costly. Salvation is free. But the Kingdom is attained only by the overcomers. All these promises may be given to us, but if we do

170

not receive them, believe them and ACT upon them, we shall not inherit them. David's own life will show us the pattern. Therefore, it is good to consider this Psalm at the very outset. Here is the vision glorious—the vision of the King and His Kingdom. To aspire unto it is blessed. But to attain it will require consecration, obedience, faith, tribulation and much warfare. It is a paradox that there is no royal way to the throne!

THE SONG OF THE INCARNATION

If David had written the eighth Psalm after the birth of Christ, it would be most masterful, most remarkable. But, when we realize that it was written a thousand years before Christ appeared on earth, it is nothing short of astounding! It is thought that David composed it in his early youth shortly after he was anointed by Samuel. Out of his heart, out of his mouth, came amazing words. "Out of the mouths of babes and sucklings hast Thou ordained strength (perfected praise)," David cried. And this revelation of God's amazing wisdom was prophetic both of himself and of the Holy Babe, the Wonder Child of the Father, Who was to be called David's son. His song continued, "Because of Thine enemies, that Thou mightest still the enemy and the avenger." David was soon to do this very thing, silencing the proud tongue of Goliath and wreaking havoc upon all the enemies of Israel. However, the greater fulfillment pointed to Christ and to Calvary.

Jesus quoted this Psalm when He made His triumphal entry into Jerusalem, and was praised by the children in the temple who cried out, "Hosanna to the son of David!" Wouldn't David have been surprised if he could have foreseen this event? He sang far better than he knew, as do all who sing by the anointing of the Holy Spirit! Our Lord on several occasions confirmed and amplified this prophecy of David. He openly thanked the Father that He had hidden His mysteries from the wise and prudent and had revealed them unto babes. He proclaimed the child the center of the Kingdom, and said that in heaven their angels do always behold the face of the Father. He sometimes referred to His disciples as children, thus revealing the spiritual significance of the child.

All during the Church age the Lord has anointed children in unusual ways and has often used them to confound sinners and unbelievers. The Spirit has revealed that in the latter days He will use many children as signs in the earth. And we rejoice in the wisdom of God, just as David did. "Oh Lord, how excellent is Thy name in all the earth!" Truly "Wisdom is justified by her children!" But we are sure David and Jesus were speaking also of those who are childlike in heart and spirit, humble, faithful and obedient unto the Father. Blessed are they in every age!

The eighth Psalm proclaims the excellency and glory of God the Creator, and David reaches rare heights of beauty and concept in this song. How he loved to invoke the sacred name of The Lord. Truly in David the Lord perfected a praise never before heard in the earth.

David had ample time and opportunity to contemplate the glories of God in the starry heavens as he watched his sheep by night. He believed that the heavenly bodies had an "ordained" ministry to man—to reveal the glory of the Creator. He was often swept into an ecstasy of praise and adoration as he viewed the splendor of the starry heavens. How insignificant man must have seemed to him by contrast! No doubt he often pondered a question which has been considered by men of every age, "What is man?" And David was given the answer to that question by divine inspiration. "Thou madest him a little lower than the angels, and hast crowned him with glory and honor. Thou madest him to have dominion over the works of Thy hands; Thou hast put all things under his feet."

He was not interested in mere philosophical theories about man, nor in a biological explanation of his physical being. It was man's relationship to God that concerned him. For David knew that God is mindful of man, as weak and insignificant as he is, and that He visits and communes with him.

Looking backward, by the enlightenment of the Spirit, David reviewed the state of Adam, as he existed with God before the fall. He sang of it with assurance. But it was of the Second Adam that his song was prophetic—of Jesus, who was to be raised up, crowned with glory and honor and given dominion over all things. David sang most surely of the incarnation to come, of Immanuel—God made man. He sang too of all those who find eternal life in Him, for they too shall be raised up in His likeness. (Acts 2:25; Heb.2:9)

We who share this glorious hope with David sing again this song of the incarnation and cry out to the Father "Help us to be child-like and ordain Thy strength in us! Perfect in us the praise that will fittingly glorify Thee! Oh Jehovah, our Adonai, how excellent is Thy name in all the earth."

"To weary travelers of every condition and at every period of history, the Psalms have been rivers of refreshment and wells of consolation. They alone have known no limitation of age, country, or form of faith. In them the spirit of controversy and the war of creeds are forgotten. Over the parched fields of theological strife the breath of the Psalms sweeps, fresh and balmy. For centuries the supplications of Christians, clothed in the language of the Psalter, have risen like incense to the altar-throne of God. In them have been expressed from age to age, the devotion and the theology of religious communions that, in all else were at deadly feud. Surviving all the changes in Church and State, in modes of thought, in habits of life, in forms of expression, the Psalms, as devotional exercises, have sunk into our hearts; as sublime poetry, they have fired our imaginations; as illustrations of human life, have arrested our minds and stored our memories."

—Rowland E. Prothero

WRITTEN IN THE SKY

When David first sang the nineteenth Psalm, a sublime song was transposed from heaven to earth. So lofty is its concept, so majestic its theme, so universal its appeal, that it is worthy of an archangel. However it was not the voice of Michael or Gabriel but that of a young shepherd who sang out vibrantly over the hills of Bethlehem: "The heavens declare the glory of God; and the firmament showeth His handiwork." Since that day, countless mortals have felt a sense of awe and wonder as they have watched a spectacular sunset or dawn; or have stood enthralled by night, gazing up into the beauty of the starry heavens. And they have sought for words with which to express their feelings and thoughts. None of them has found more eloquent words than David's. The literal Hebrew gives them to us in this way:

> "The heavens are telling the glory of God;
> The firmament displaying the work of His hands;
> Day unto day telleth forth speech,
> Night unto night breatheth out knowledge."

It is believed that David sang these phrases during his youth, while he was still tending his father's sheep. The long days and nights spent outdoors afforded an opportunity for sustained worship and contemplation. There is no suggestion in this Psalm of the sufferings and struggles of his later years. It is the song of a soul "en rapport" with the Creator and at peace with all men. The eighth Psalm and the twenty-ninth Psalm are thought to be from the same period. Dr. MacClaren says of them: "They are unlike David's later songs in the almost entire absence of personal references or of signs of the varied experiences of human life. They reveal a self-forgetful contemplation and tranquility which must have been outpoured from a young heart free from pain, far from men and very near to God. Common to them all is the peculiar manner of looking upon nature, so uniform in David's Psalms, so unlike most descriptive poetry. David can smite out a picture in a phrase. But he does not care to paint landscapes. Creation is to him neither a subject for poetical description, nor for scientific study. It is the garment of God! The apocalypse of the heavenly!"

This sacramentalizing of all nature compares with the poetry and songs of St. Francis and his brethren. Everything in nature stirred their hearts to worship and adore the Creator, and revealed something of His heart and nature to them.

How very Davidic was Francis! Both were troubadours of the great King. Both saw the unveiling of God in sun and earth and sky and sea. His Word was revealed in everything and everyone! Paul was attuned to this concept when he wrote, "Thou, Lord, in the beginning has laid the foundation of the earth; and the heavens are the works of Thine hands: they shall perish; but Thou remainest; and they all shall wax old as doth a garment; and as a vesture shalt Thou fold them up..." (Heb. 1:10-12) "For the invisible things of Him from the foundation of the world are clearly seen, being understood by the things that are made, even His eternal power and Godhead..." (Rom. 1:20) We seldom think of Paul as a Psalmist. But he was truly a poet and a singer. His instruction to the Church to bring forth the Word in psalms and hymns and spiritual songs was born out of his own rich experience. And indeed the Holy Spirit sang in him a

NEW SONG—a song of grace and love, a heavenly epithalamium for Christ and His Bride!

Some Bible scholars question the connection between the first half of the nineteenth Psalm with the last part. But David never doubted the relationship between God's Word in Creation and His Word in Scripture. "Forever, O Lord, Thy Word is *settled in heaven.*" Yes, and *written in heaven* as well! The ancients read God's Word in the stars and found it very revealing. The Magi followed His sign in the sky and it led them to Jesus. Primeval Astronomy teaches us that the entire story of redemption is recorded in the signs of the Zodiac.

C.H. Spurgeon comments as follows: "David's early life was devoted to the study of God's two great books—nature and Scripture; and he had so thoroughly entered into the spirit of these two—the only volumes in his library—that he was able with a devout criticism to compare and contrast them, magnifying the excellency of the Author as seen in both. How foolish and wicked are those who instead of accepting the two sacred tomes, and delighting to behold the same divine hand in each, spend all their wits in endeavoring to find discrepancies and contradictions. He is wisest who reads both the world-book and the Word-book as two volumes of the same work. The world-book has three leaves—heaven, earth and sea, of which heaven is the first and most glorious. By its aid we are able to see the beauties of the other two."

Not only did David sing of the Written Word, but also of the Living Word—Christ Jesus. Paul quotes these words of David in Romans 10:18. And truly Jesus is readily seen as the spiritual Sun (Son) coming forth out of His wedding chamber, rejoicing as a strong man as He runs His race. How often has the Holy Spirit quickened these verses in relationship to His Endtime plan. In Psalm forty-five we behold the King, prepared for His marriage and the Marriage Supper of the Lamb. Then, in the nineteenth Psalm we see Him coming forth out of His wedding chamber, clothed in majesty and power. The Word is carried to every tongue and tribe and nation. And soon the knowledge of the Lord covers the earth as the waters cover the sea. Already His anointed ones have had foretastes as well as previews of this great consummation of the age.

Even in this present time there is a very real sense in which this Word is being fulfilled. Quoting again from Spurgeon: "God's way of grace is sublime and broad and full of His glory. It has been proclaimed in a measure to the whole world. And in due time it shall be more completely published to all peoples. Jesus, like a sun, dwells in the midst of revelation, tabernacling among men in all His brightness, rejoicing as the Bridegroom of His Church, revealing Himself to His own. He wars like a champion for their deliverance. He makes a circuit of mercy, blessing the very ends of the earth. And there are no seeking souls however degraded or depraved who are denied the comforting warmth and benediction of His love."

Another writer has interpreted this word in a most interesting way: "As the material sun, through the twelve signs of the Zodiac, goes forth from the uttermost parts of the heaven, and returns to the end of it again; in like sort, the spiritual Son of Righteousness, by the twelve Apostles, as by the twelve signs, has been borne around the world, that He might be not only 'the glory of His people Israel,' but, 'a light to lighten the Gentiles' as well; so that 'all the ends of the earth' might see the salvation of our God."

David's intense love for the Written Word is revealed in the latter portion of the Psalm. He delights in singing of its perfection, its surety, justice, purity, power and truth. He declares that it brings the believer conversion, wisdom, rejoicing, enlightenment and righteousness. He finds the Word to be more precious than gold and sweeter than honey to the taste. Such enthusiastic praise of the Scriptures in the heart of a youth is indeed amazing!

How quickly David turns from extolling the Word to examining his own heart, praying for cleansing and instruction. His closing words are as famous and as well loved as the opening verses of this Psalm. "Let the words of my mouth and the meditations of my heart be acceptable in Thy sight, O Lord, my strength and my redeemer." Not of the universe does he sing now, but of his own heart. This song has spanned the distance between God's macrocosm in creation and His microcosm in man's heart. And David knew of a surety that the latter was of more importance to Him than all the starry heavens!

GOD SAVE THE KING!

Although the commentators are not agreed about the author of the twentieth Psalm, most of them attribute it to David. It is truly Davidic in character. It was likely written after the Temple worship was established. The King was about to lead his armies forth against some aggressor. Some say that the enemies were the Ammonites and Syrians, mentioned in 2 Samuel. These nations used horses and chariots in warfare, a thing forbidden to the Israelites. Before going to the battle, David brings his men to the temple, and they are set in array, banners flying, while he goes in to offer sacrifices to the Lord.

It is a Messianic Psalm, given to the Chief Musician, according to the title. And it is in a dialogue, as is the twenty-fourth. The suggested order:

> Verses 1-3—The prayers of the people who have assembled.
> 4—The words of the High Priest.
> 5—David and his attendants. Last part spoken by the
> Priest.
> 6—Priest after sacrifice was given.
> 7,8—David and his men.
> 9—Congregation.

This Psalm has been widely used for national holidays, Coronations and other special events connected with warfare. It was much loved and quoted by the early as well as later saints, particularly in reference to spiritual warfare. St. Patrick quoted it when he defied the Druids and dared to celebrate Easter service at the time of their "holy fire" ceremonies. The king sent soldiers and horses and chariots for him, and he quoted verse 5 all the way he had to travel. By the Word of the Lord he overcame them and established Christian worship in Ireland.

The people of the Commonwealth of Great Britain have a special claim upon this Psalm, for it is the origin of their national Hymn, "God Save The King (Queen)!" But we in America have an even greater claim, I feel, because out of their hymn our own "America" was born. And in it we have a line that expresses the true meaning of verse 9: "Protect us by Thy might, Great God our King!" The Spirit has given us this Psalm again and again, always with Christ the King, and His Kingdom, in view. One translation here reads, "O Lord, save the King, and answer us in the day when we cry!" Another is, "O Jehovah, give victory unto the King, hear our cry!"

Every verse of this Psalm has been given special emphasis in our day. The Lord has indeed heard our prayers in this day of worldwide trouble; He has taught us the power of His Sacred Name to defend us; He has sent us help from His sanctuary (on earth and in heaven) again and again. He has strengthened us out of Zion, accepted our offerings and sacrifices, both material and spiritual, and granted us our heart's desire, fulfilling our hopes in Him. He has taught us the way of praise and rejoicing. He has demonstrated His constant protection of His anointed ones. The saving strength of His right hand has often been in evidence. We indeed remember and rehearse the name of the Lord. And again and again we see the enemy fall to the dust, while we are raised to stand in worship and victory before the Lord. Wonderful! Great is our King and His Kingdom!

"If your praise at times seems weak, remember that if you cannot offer strong shouts and high songs, you can still keep breathing forth praise and blessing out of your heart's desire toward God."

THE SHEPHERD PSALM

The twenty-third Psalm is without a doubt the most loved and famous poem ever written. It reflects David's boyhood life and his earliest concept of God. Regardless of when it may have been written, it is definitely David's first and greatest Psalm. "Out of the mouths of babes and sucklings, Thou has perfected praise." C.H. Spurgeon has highly praised this Psalm in *The Treasury of David*. He says:

"This is David's heavenly pastoral; a surpassing ode, which none of the daughters of music can excel. Sitting under a spreading tree, with his flock around him, like Bunyan's shepherd boy in the Valley of Humiliation, we picture David singing this unrivaled pastoral with a heart as full of gladness as it could hold; or, if the Psalm be a product of his after years, we are sure that his soul returned in contemplation to the lonely waterbrooks which rippled among the pastures of the wilderness, where in early days he had been wont to dwell. This is the pearl of Psalms whose soft and pure radiance delights every eye. Of this delightful song it may be affirmed that its piety and poetry are equal, its sweetness and its spirituality are unsurpassed.

"It has been said that what the nightingale is among birds, that is this divine ode among the Psalms, for it has sung sweetly in the ear of many a mourner in his night of weeping, and has bidden him hope for a morning of joy. I will venture to compare it also to the lark, which sings as it mounts, and mounts as it sings, until it is out of sight, and even then is not out of hearing."

To come to know the Jehovah of the Old Testament as a tender, loving, personal shepherd, required the heart of a child—a child enlightened by the Holy Spirit. To the Hebrews, God was a warrior, judge, lawgiver, ruler and disciplinarian. He was strong and stern, and was to be feared even more than loved. It took David to see beyond God's majesty, into His heart of compassion and tender affection. He was the first to say or sing, "The Lord is *my* Shepherd." And David knew from first-hand experience how much the shepherd loves his sheep, how intimately he lives with them, how devotedly he cares for them, how valiantly he protects them, and how ready he is to sacrifice his own life for them. Rightly does the twenty-third Psalm follow the heart-rending twenty-second, in which Jesus is seen laying down His life for His own. It has been said that the twenty-second is "The Good Shepherd" Psalm; the twenty-third "The Great Shepherd" Psalm; and the twenty-fourth is "The Chief Shepherd" Psalm.

In Jacob's dying prophecy, the Lord was referred to as "the Shepherd and Stone (Rock) of Israel." How remarkable that these two figures of speech were revived in David centuries later; for up until the time of David, only one other, himself a shepherd, had apparently seen the Lord as a Shepherd. (Num. 27:17) To the Egyptians "every shepherd was an abomination." Even among the Israelites, shepherds were not particularly honored, though they were respected. David's revelation is all the more unusual because of this. How indebted we are to him for this sweet song of childlike simplicity and wonder!

The prophets Isaiah and Jeremiah used this same concept again and again. And Jesus Himself confirmed and augmented it in the 10th chapter of John, and in the parable of the ninety and nine.

No more touching self-portrait of Jesus has been left to us. Again, in the closing of John, we find Jesus telling Peter to tend and feed His flock like a shepherd. Both Peter and Paul referred to Jesus as The Shepherd, and to His pastors as under-shepherds. Even in the closing book of the Bible, the Lord is pictured as both the Lamb and the Shepherd, leading His sheep beside the living waters.

Although we may have read the twenty-third Psalm dozens of times, memorized it, studied it, and listened to many sermons about it, there are always new gems of truth to be garnered from it. One of our number shared with us an inspiring revelation once given to her. She had noticed that in verse one, David referred to Jehovah as the Shepherd. And then as she read on, the Spirit showed her that all the compound names of Jehovah are hidden in this short song.

Jehovah-Rohi: The Lord, my Shepherd. "The Lord is my Shepherd."

Jehovah-Jireh: The Lord will provide. "I shall not want."

Jehovah-Shalom: The Lord is peace. "He leadeth me beside still waters."

Jehovah-Rapha: The Lord our healer. "He restoreth my soul."

Jehovah-Tsidkenu: The Lord our righteousness. "Paths of righteousness."

Jehovah-Nissi: The Lord my banner (protection). "In the presence of mine enemies."

Jehovah-M'Kaddesh: The Lord which sanctifies. "He anointeth my head."

Jehovah-Shammah: The Lord is there. "I shall dwell in the house of the Lord forever."

Although men of various religions, or none, have learned to love and claim the Shepherd Psalm, yet properly it applies only to the redeemed—in other words, to sheep. It is not wild animals that the Shepherd tends; not goats or asses—but sheep. And in the story of the ninety and nine it is a lost sheep that the Shepherd goes to find. Only those who have been born again, receiving the new nature of the Lamb of God, can properly be called sheep.

In the first few verses we find a picture of the two-fold life of the child of God—contemplative and active. And contemplative is mentioned first. He does not lead us forth at once into activity and service, but into *rest*! In green pastures we are fed upon the Word. At still waters we drink and lie down. All this is a type of prayer and waiting on the Lord. It reminds us of Isaiah 40:28-31. It is they who learn how to rest in the Lord, to wait upon Him, to worship and contemplate—that are renewed and lifted up in strength.

The next portion depicts activity—paths of righteousness, witnessing and serving. Then comes the Valley of the Shadow of Death—a pilgrimage involving suffering, danger, loneliness and testing. There is also correction and protection; a gradual maturing into sonship; after all these comes the greater feasting with the Lord—the table in the wilderness, the anointing, the full cup! And all this is crowned with eternal goodness, mercy and rest in the Father's House.

From Henry Ward Beecher we have taken this closing tribute: "Blessed be the day the twenty-third Psalm was born! Like a singing angel it goes its way into all the lands, singing in the language of every nation, driving away trouble by the impulses of the air which its tongue moves with divine power. This 'pilgrimage' has charmed more griefs to rest than all the philosophies of the world. It has remanded to their dungeon more felon thoughts, more black doubts, more thieving sorrow, than there are sands on the seashore. It has comforted the noble host of the poor. It has sung courage to the army of the disappointed. It has poured balm and consolation into the hearts of the sick and captive. Dying soldiers have died easier as it was read to them. It has visited the prisoner and broken his chains. It has made the dying Christian slave freer than his master. Nor is its work done. It will go on singing through all the generations of time. Nor will it fold its wings until the last pilgrim is safe, and time ended. Then it shall fly back to the bosom of God, whence it issued."

DAVID'S GLORIA

Among David's most exalted gems, the Twenty-ninth Psalm shines out with striking beauty and power. Here is a jewel fit for the diadem of the King of Heaven! Because it depicts David's reaction to an electric storm, we might name it his "thunder and lightning" song. But we have chosen to call it his Gloria, since its theme is "the glory of the Lord" and "The God of Glory." It seems certain that it was composed during his pastoral days and is fit companion for the Eighth and Nineteenth Psalms.

A thunderstorm is one of nature's most dramatic performances. And both men and animals are impressed and affected by it, especially if they meet it out in the open. Even before the storm begins, animals sense its approach and tend to become agitated. When it breaks, they will vary in reactions: some will be oppressed or frightened; while others may become animated or even exultant, as the case may be. Men too vary in their reactions. The more primitive races believe that their gods roar at them in the thunder and flash their weapons in lightning strokes of anger. Poets and artists thrill to the beauty and music. Scientists ponder its secrets. But David, the artist and worshiper, felt in the storm a great stirring of his emotions toward God. In its roar he heard a call to high and holy worship. In its flashes he caught glimpses of the lightning around the Throne. The physical power displayed was to him but a cloak, an outward form of the spiritual power of the Creator. In his day man had not yet learned how to reach into the skies and harness the mysterious energy that activates a thunderstorm. But we, who live three thousand years after David's time, enjoy the wonders of such knowledge and realize that electricity is a symbol of the power of God.

David doubtless often witnessed such storms while tending his sheep. At some time or other he may have experienced one while in the mountains. The majesty and wonder he felt impressed him deeply and found expression in a song which has lived through centuries. Perhaps he had seen lightning strike one of the trees, kindling a fire—an altar-fire for David's ecstatic heart! In any case, David lifted up his voice in a resonant call to worship: "Give unto the Lord, O ye mighty, give unto the Lord glory and strength!" In its original version this phrase refers directly to the angelic hosts above, the "angels that excel in strength." David is beside himself with joy, the Spirit of Sonship rises in his heart. He is elevated to the courts above and assumes the role of a chief singer and worshiper—his eternal vocation in God. "Give unto the Lord the glory due unto His name; worship the Lord in the beauty of holiness." Here is high inspiration—great poetic art! And here is a line that has lived on, age after age, as precious to us who worship today as to David when it was first born in his heart. When the Spirit reiterates it in our hearts and mouths, we too are lifted up to the Sanctuary in the Heavens. And we are reminded of what Paul wrote of it in Hebrews, and John in The Revelation. But David had never read their words. He sang by the direct inspiration of the Spirit.

Each short sentence is like a clap of thunder. And seven times the voice of Jehovah thunders! A majestic prelude to the seven thunders of the Apocalypse! Alexander MacLaren has written beautifully of this Psalm as follows: "Its very structure reproduces in sound an echo of the rolling peals reverberating among the hills... Seven times the roar shakes the world. In the short clauses, with their uniform structure, the pause between, and the recurrence of the same initial words, we hear the successive peals, the silence that parts them, and the monotony of their unvaried sound. Thrice we have the reverberation rolling through the sky among the hills, imitated by clauses which repeat previous ones. The range and effects of the storm are vividly painted. It is first, 'On the waters,' which may possibly mean the Mediterranean, but more probably, 'the waters that are above the firmament,' and so depicts the clouds as gathering high in the air. Then it comes down with a crash on the northern mountains, splintering the gnarled cedars... Onward it sweeps—or rather, perhaps, it is all around the Psalmist; and even while he hears the voice rolling from the farthest north, the extreme south echoes the roar. The awful voice shakes the wilderness. (Some render this 'whirls in circles'—alluding to sandstorms in the desert.) As far south as Kadesh (probably Petra) the tremor spreads, and away in the forests of Edom the wild creatures in their terror slip their calves, and the oaks are scathed and stripped of their leafy honors. And all the while, like a mighty diapason, sounding on through the tumult the voices of the sons of God in the heavenly temple are heard proclaiming, 'Glory!'

"The Psalm closes with lofty words of confidence, built on the story of the past, as well as the contemplation of the present... As the tempest rolls away, spent and transient, the sunshine streams out anew from the softened blue over a freshened world, and every raindrop on the leaves twinkles into diamond light, and the end of the Psalm is like the after brightness; 'The Lord will bless His people with peace.'"

This magnificent Gloria has been frequently impressed upon many who have received the Latter Day outpouring of the Spirit.

Those who are being prepared as "sons of glory" sometimes find themselves rapt in exultation similar to that which David felt. They receive new concepts of the beauty and wonder of the worship of the Sanctuary. They hear the voice of the Lord in the thunder, the wind, the sea, the sky—and they respond with praise akin to David's. They know that one of these days, "The Lord shall utter His voice before His army," and all the earth shall be shaken. They expectantly await the seven thunders that are to announce the consummation of the age. And they rejoice in the certainty that "the glory of the Lord shall be revealed and all flesh shall see it together." Their greatest concern is to worship the Lord in the beauty—not duty—of holiness, and to give Him at all times the glory due to His holy name! For they behold Him already seated and crowned—the King eternal and immortal!

THE THIRSTING SOUL

The commentators do not agree about the authorship of the Forty-second Psalm, but most of them attribute it to David. It is truly Davidic in character. Its poetic quality marks its author as a supreme poet. It abounds in Davidic symbols and expressions: the hart, streams of water, God the Rock, the Living God, the multitude on holy day, etc. The Syriac version says that it was composed by David in exile. And it is generally believed that he wrote it while in exile after Absalom's rebellion. During this time, of course, he had no access to the beautiful Tabernacle worship which he had established in Jerusalem. His longing for the Ark, the songs and music of the Lord, the intense and concentrated worship of the assembly, is depicted herein. Note that his lamentation is not for the loss of the throne, or the honors of the kingdom, but for the high and holy worship he has experienced in the Sanctuary.

It is a Maschil, an instructive ode, for the sons of Korah—the honored singers of chief songs. It is intended for public worship and use. Spurgeon believes this Psalm indisputably Davidic. He comments as follows: "Debarred from public worship, David is heartsick. Ease he did not seek, honor he did not covet. But the enjoyment of worship and holy communion with God was an urgent need of his soul. He viewed it not merely as the sweetest of all luxuries, but as an absolute necessity, like water to a stag. Like the parched traveler in the wilderness, whose skin bottle is empty, and who finds the wells dry, he must drink or die—he must have his God or faint... As the hart brays, so David's soul prays! His heart heaves, his bosom palpitates, his whole frame is convulsed, like one who gasps for breath, panting after long running."

Here is a picture of desire for worship that cannot be surpassed anywhere in the Scripture. How pale and sickly do our own aspirations and longings appear in the light of such extreme thirst and passion!

Even though none of us has ever been put through the outward suffering, persecution, betrayal and banishment that David experienced, this Psalm has been a source of comfort and strength in many a desperate hour. Most of us have been permitted to share a degree, at least, of the rejection, enmity, opposition and loneliness herein depicted. We too have felt the floods of darkness and death sweep over our souls, and we have been battered by their cruel waves. At other times we have been taken into the wilderness experience and have fainted in the drought. We have known what it is to pant for the Spirit. Our tears have been poured out. Our God has seemed lost or far away. At such times this song has brought instruction, inspiration, and strength to us. We are not to remain cast down; we are to *pour out* our soul; we are to *praise* the Lord— even in such straights. We are not to become numb with grief, but to *remember* His past blessings. We are to continue to *sing* and *pray* in the night seasons and throughout the long exhausting days. We are not to be overcome by our enemy and his taunts—but to *hope* and continue to *praise.*

Yes, this song is indubitably a song of David. And it is believed that the Forty-third Psalm is a continuation of it. With confidence David looks forward to restoration at the altar of God, to a renewal of his song and joy in the Lord. It is clear that David did experience such joyful restoration and that he shall dwell in the house of the Lord all the days of his life. And so shall we, yes, so shall we.

Because this Psalm is so beautifully translated in the Knox Version, I want to share it with you: "O God, my soul longs for Thee, as a deer for running water; my whole soul thirsts for God, the strong, the living God; shall I never again make my pilgrimage into God's presence? Morning and evening, my diet is tears! Daily I must listen to the taunt, 'Where is thy God now?' Memories come back to me yet, melting my heart; I am back at God's house, His majestic tabernacle, amid the cries of joy and thanksgiving, and all the noise of holy day. (Or, 'I led the crowd in the rejoicing on holy day.') Soul, art thou still downcast? Wilt thou never be at peace? Wait for God's help; I will not cease to cry out in thankfulness, my champion and my God.

"In my sad mood I will think of Thee, here in this land of Jordan and Hermon, here on Mizar mountain. One depth makes answer to another amid the roar of the floods Thou sendest; wave after wave, crest after crest overwhelms me. Such mercy the Lord has shown me while the day lasted; and have I no song for Him, here in the night, no prayer to the God who is life for me? Thou art my stronghold, I will tell Him; hast Thou never a thought for me? Must I go mourning, with enemies pressing me hard; racked by the ceaseless taunts of my persecutors, 'Where is thy God now?' Soul, art thou still downcast? Wilt thou never be at peace? Wait for God's help; I will not cease to cry out in thankfulness, my champion and my God."

"The book of Psalms contains the whole music of the heart of man, swept by the hand of his Maker. In it are gathered the lyrical burst of his tenderness, the moan of his penitence, the pathos of his sorrow, the triumph of his victory, the despair of his defeat, the firmness of his confidence, the rapture of his assured hope. In it is presented the anatomy of all parts of the human soul; in it are collected, sunrise and sunset; birth and death, promise and fulfillment—the whole drama of humanity."

THE CRY OF THE LORD'S FLOCK

A positive identification of the author of the Forty-fourth Psalm is not possible. But it is generally agreed that it was written by the author of the Forty-second. Davidic characteristics are most marked. But the occasions bringing about its composition cannot be located. It is possible that it is only partially factual and mostly prophetic. The twenty-second Psalm was of this type. David, by the Spirit, could have looked into the future and seen the national distress and calamity he describes.

This Psalm was a great favorite with the fathers of the early Church. They believed that it was composed for the Church, far more than for literal Israel, and that only in the Church were the terrible sufferings it describes fulfilled. Since Paul quotes a portion of it in this connection, this interpretation can readily be understood. We who live in this era know that time and time again Israel suffered the terrible defeat and captivity herein described. But Israel usually suffered for *disobedience.* The Church, on the other hand, suffered far greater martyrdom—while in *obedience* and fellowship with Christ. It is this type of defeat that David is singing about—the *seeming* failure of God to deliver His faithful followers.

"Thou art King, O God, command deliverances..." we cry. Although the Lord has invincible power to protect and deliver, yet there are times when the Lord seems to sleep or be indifferent to our dangers and sufferings. This is true in the life of the individual and true in the life of the Church. There have been many seasons when He has seen fit not to spare His most faithful followers intense suffering and even martyrdom. In our own day we have known of the terrible persecutions of Christians in various nations. Many of these were more dedicated than we. They served the same Lord. Yet they were not delivered or spared. The mystery of why God miraculously delivers some of His saints from physical harm and yet allows others to become victims of the forces of evil is still baffling men.

We all thrill to the marvelous way the Lord delivered the Hebrew Children from the fiery furnace. But the Spirit has given greater emphasis to their *attitude* than to the *deliverance.* And what was their attitude? They said to the king, "Our God whom we serve is able to deliver us from the burning fiery furnace, and He *will* deliver us out of thine hand, O king. *But if not...* we will not serve thy gods." They fully believed in the power and willingness of God to deliver. Yet they were resolved to be faithful to Him if, for some reason unknown to them, He failed to do so. They were sure that they would be taken out of the evil king's hand either by miracle or by death. And this has been the settled attitude of Christian martyrs for centuries.

This blessed Psalm has been quickened by the Spirit at various times in a variety of ways in our own experience. We too have become "as sheep led to the slaughter"—members of that "flock of the slaughter" of which the Psalmist sang. The death we die "all the day long" may never be physical but, instead, a death to *self.* Our sufferings and breakings may be unseen, unknown to others, yet nonetheless real and painful. We too may find that the Lord tarries long, as though in sleep, before He rises for our deliverance. In all these things, may we, by His grace, not "deal falsely with His covenant," nor be "turned back." May our steps never decline from His way. These sufferings which seem so strange and futile to us are actually a part of the heritage of all saints—both in the Old Testament and in the New. And all who are in the flock of the Lord will find that sacrifices and suffering are included in the Great Plan. Although the Psalmist does not reach a place of triumphant faith in this song, he does indeed prove faithful through severe testing, relying on the mercies of the Lord.

Centuries later, after the outpouring of the Holy Spirit, the Apostles of our Lord sang the antiphonal to this sad song. Its theme was, "In all these things we are more than conquerors!" They made it clear that it is an honor and glory to share in the sufferings of Christ, and that "present sufferings are not worthy to be compared with the glory that shall be revealed," in Him. They also understood that not only are we *purified* through fiery trials, we are also made *fruitful.* The blood of the martyrs is indeed the seed of the Church. And no sacrifice or suffering for Christ's sake is ever in vain. To these truths the blessed Holy Spirit witnesses again and again, as He resolves our own sad songs into paeans of praise and victory.

"In the Psalms the vast hosts of suffering humanity have found, from the time of Jonah to the present day, the deepest expression of their hopes and fears. As our Lord Himself died with the words of a Psalm upon His lips, so the first martyr, Stephen, used the words thus hallowed. So also, in prison at Philippi, Paul and Silas encouraged themselves by singing Psalms throughout the night. It was by the Psalms that the anguish, wrung from tortured lips on the cross, at the stake, on the scaffold and in the dungeon, has been healed and solaced. Strong in the strength that they impart, young boys and timid girls have risen from their knees in the breathless suspense of the amphitheater, thronged with its quivering multitudes, and boldly faced the lions."

—Rowland E. Prothero

THE KING'S CROWN JEWELS

The One hundred-tenth Psalm, with its seven short verses, was esteemed by many of the early writers to be the Crown of all the Psalms. The ancients term this Psalm, "The Sun of our Faith," "The Treasure of the Holy Writ." Martin Luther designated it as the "Crown Psalm" and said that it was worthy to be overlaid with precious jewels.

Edward Reynolds, writing of it in the sixteenth century has this to say of it: "This Psalm is one of the fullest and most compendious prophecies of the person and offices of Christ in the entire Old Testament, and is so full of fundamental truth, that I shall not shun to call it, 'The prophet David's creed.' The doctrine of the Trinity is in the first words, 'Jehovah said unto my Adonai.' The Father is consecrating the Son, by the Holy Spirit, to be David's Lord. We have following this: the incarnation, the sufferings, the completed work of Calvary, His resurrection, ascension, intercession and finally His Holy Body, Zion. There is also a glimpse of the day of His wrath and the time of His final triumph."

Does this beautiful Crown Jewel, so appreciated and admired by the saints of old, have a special message to us of the Twentieth

Century, as we look into its shining glory? In the King James version it reads, "Thy people shall be willing in the day of Thy power, in the beauties of holiness, from the womb of the morning; Thou hast the dew of thy youth." In the American Revised Version it is rendered: "Thy people offer themselves willingly (margin—free-will offerings) in the day of Thy power (margin—army.) In holy array. Out of the womb of the morning. Thou hast the dew of Thy youth (margin— Thy youth are to Thee as dew.)"

This verse has been so often spoken to our hearts, and with such emphasis by the Spirit, that we have been convinced that it refers to the Latter Day outpourings of the Spirit and the mighty manifestations of the Lord in the midst of His people. How it thrilled our hearts to make a search back into the bygone days and find that those who were attuned to the voice of the Spirit in those days were given a similar revelation.

First of all we will quote from C.H. Spurgeon. In his comments he writes as follows: "'The Lord shall send forth the rod of Thy strength out of Zion.' It is in and through the Church that, for the present, the power of the Messiah is known. Jehovah has given to Jesus all authority in the midst of His people, whom he rules with His royal scepter. And this power goes forth with divine energy from the Church for the ingathering of the elect and the subduing of all evil. We need to pray for the sending out of the rod of divine strength! It was by his rod that Moses smote the Egyptians and wrought wonders for Israel. And even so, whenever the Lord Jesus sends forth the rod of His strength our spiritual enemies are overcome."

This promise began to be fulfilled at Pentecost, and it continues even to this day, and shall yet have a grander fulfillment. O God of eternal might, let the strength of our Lord Jesus be more clearly seen, and let the nations see it as coming forth out of the midst of Thy people, Zion, the place of Thy abode! We look for a clearer manifestation of His almighty power in these Latter days. "Thy people shall be willing in the day of Thy power." In consequence of His sending forth the rod of His strength, many will come forward to enlist under the banner of our Priest-King. This metaphor may be enlarged upon, for as the dew has a sparkling beauty, so these willing armies will have a holy excellence and charm about them. From Spurgeon we quote again: "Let the Word of the Lord be preached with divine unction, and the chosen of the Lord will respond to it like troops on the day of the mustering of the armies; arrayed by grace in shining uniforms of holiness. The realization of this day of power during the time of the Lord's tarrying is that which we should constantly pray for; and we may legitimately expect it, since He sits in the seat of power and authority, and puts forth His strength according to His Word. 'My Father worketh hitherto, and I work.'"

Quoting now from Alexander MacLaren: "The subjects of the Priest-King are willing soldiers. In accordance with the military tone of the whole Psalm, our text describes the subjects as an army. The word rendered 'power' and rightly so, is derived from that which we translate 'army.' We do not refer to 'powers' but to 'troops' or 'forces.' 'The day of Thy Power' may also be rendered, 'the day of Thy might,' 'The day of Thy army!' That is literally 'the day when Thou dost muster Thy forces and go forth to battle; having set them in array.' The King is going forth to conquest, but He goes not alone. Behind Him come His faithful followers, all pressing on with willing hearts and high courage."

The conquering King, of whom this Psalm sings, is a Priest forever; and He is followed by an army of priests. The soldiers gathered in the day of this muster—with high courage and willing devotion, ready to fling away their lives—are not clad in mail, but in priestly robes, like those who compassed Jericho with the ark for their standard and trumpets for their weapons. "Thou has the dew of Thy youth." Youth used here is a collective noun, equivalent to "young men." The host of His soldier-subjects is described as a band of young warriors, whom He leads in their fresh strength and countless numbers and gleaming beauty, as the dew of the morning. As the Revised Version says, "Thy youth are to Thee as dew." It is a symbol of the refreshing which the weary world will receive from the conquests and presence of the King and His host. Another prophecy gives us the same emblem speaking of Israel being "in the midst of many people as dew from the Lord." (Micah 5:7)

"He shall drink of the brook in the way." These words were understood by Junius to mean, "He shall steadily press on to victory as generals of energy act, who, in pursuing routed forces, stay not to indulge themselves in meat or drink." We are inclined to take Gideon as the type that best expresses the thought. Pressing on to victory, Messiah, like Gideon, passes over Jordan and shall not desist till all is won. "A short work He will make in the earth, He will cut it short in righteousness."

Surely it ought to stir our hearts anew, as we see the day dawning of which these men of old dreamed and wrote. The day of His power! May we be among the willing people through whom He shall work His mighty works to the ends of the earth! We read in the Song of Solomon (6:12): "Or ever I was aware, my soul made me like the chariots of Aminidab." The marginal note reads, "Set me on the chariots of my willing people." Or, as another version states, "My princely people." Here too is a picture of the Lord going forth in the midst of His princely (praying), willing (consecrated) people, going swiftly in power and salvation to the ends of the earth.

The King and His Crown Jewels are ours, and we are His, for glorious conquest. "Now shall He be great to the ends of the earth!" Remember that this promise on which we base our faith was made by Jehovah, the Eternal One, to our Lord Adonai, His only begotten Son. The Father will keep His word to His Son. He shall see the travail of His soul and be satisfied. He shall see His enemies become His footstool.

> From the womb of the morning
> With the dew of Thy youth,
> Thy people shall rise, Lord,
> In the light of Thy truth,
> And shall willingly offer
> Themselves unto Thee—
> On the day of Thy power and victory.
> Oh hail our great High Priest!
> O hail our glorious King!
> In the beauty of holiness
> Our praise to Thee we bring,
> As we willingly offer
> Ourselves unto Thee—
> Lead us on in Thy conquest to victory!

—F.M.

HIS APPEARING

The Golden Candlestick

P lease remember as you read this booklet that it was written approximately forty years ago by various members of the GOLDEN CANDLESTICK company. Each had come from a different Church background, but all had a burning desire to know Jesus in a deeper way. They were drawn together in an intercessory prayer group which became the GOLDEN CANDLESTICK.

These articles and poems, written so long ago, are a fore-showing of our Lord's desire in these last days. He made Himself known then, and He makes Himself known now, to those who are "waiting and watching for Him."

Pour out your soul even unto death,
His life you shall receive;
A living death—a dying life,
For all who to Him cleave.

When you are dead to self and sin
And Christ, The LIFE, in you—tho'
You still live, yet you are dead—
His Life is brought to view.

So let Him live His life thru you
His life poured out again.
For first the world must see Him, thus
And then He'll come to reign.

—M.J.P.

APOCALYPSE

Out of the east I beheld Him rise
Sweeping thro' the everlasting portals
Lift up your heads, O ye golden gates—
He arises!—Potentate Immortal!
His wings, a-tipped with living fire,
      Are outspread from earth to Heaven;
      His right arm is outstretched in power,
      And the stars in His hand are seven!

His feet are aglow—as burnished brass,
His eyes flash with Love's pure flame,
His hair, as white as snowy wool,
His shining countenance doth frame!
He is the first and the last;
      Alpha and Omega—Aleph and Tau—
      Which was—which is—and is to come—
      The Almighty whom Daniel saw!

His voice, as the sound of many waters,
Swells, like a sea, to deafening roar!
Heaven and earth are all a-tremble
And are moved as in the days of yore—
When He descended unto Israel
      'Mid lightnings the heavens were bowed,
      His footsteps shook the barren wilderness—
      As He marched before His people in a cloud.

He that hath eyes, let him watch and see!
He that hath ears, let him harken and hear!
In the midst of the golden candlesticks He walks,

And unto His people He doth NOW appear!
Unto His messengers He doth now speak,
    And His tongue is as a two-edged sword—
    O Living Church of the Living God—
    Hear the Living Word of the Lord!

                            —F.M.

HIS APPEARING

"He shall appear to your joy." (Isa. 65:5)

"Christ having been offered... will appear a second time, not carrying any burden of sin nor to deal with sin, but to bring to full salvation those who are eagerly, constantly and patiently waiting for and expecting Him." (Heb. 9:28 Amp.)

The appearing or revelation of Jesus Christ in the members of His mystical Body is a glorious earnest and foretaste of His full incarnation in His corporeal Body. It is basically taught by the entire New Testament, and especially emphasized by the teachings of St. Paul: "Christ IN you the hope of glory." "All we, beholding as in a mirror the glory of the Lord, are changed into the SAME IMAGE, from glory to glory, even as by the Spirit of God. "For whom He did foreknow He also did predestinate to be conformed to the IMAGE of His Son." (Rom. 8:29)

From the beginning of the new dispensation in Christ, it was the Father's plan that in every generation His Son should APPEAR and be MANIFEST on earth in the sanctified bodies of the redeemed. The Father desires, not an imitation of Christ by mere servants and followers, but an *incarnation* of Jesus Christ in His seed—the sons of God! He, indeed, was "cut off out of the land of the living," yet, by means of indwelling the bodies of those who are willing to present themselves as living sacrifices, "He shall see His seed. He shall prolong His days."

He has no body but our bodies through whom He may work. "Present your body a living sacrifice!" Why? Because He wants to live again, work again, speak again, be SEEN again, in the earth! This is the great desire of His heart!

The early Church grasped this great truth—and the ACTS OF THE APOSTLES might be more truly entitled THE ACTS OF JESUS CHRIST IN THE APOSTLES. Christ was so manifest in St. Paul that he became a veritable "God-man" to many, yet he always declared, "Not I, but Christ who liveth in me." There is a tradition that a young virgin, who was about to be martyred, glanced at the Apostle on her way to the cruel stake; and saw not Paul, but Jesus! He unveiled Himself to her in such glory that she was strengthened to die a heroic death.

It was not uncommon, in those days, for Jesus to be seen in different members of His Ecclesia. And sometimes this occurred quite openly. Another legend related that when a devoted woman follower was being tortured, her body altered in a strange manner, and not only believers, but unbelievers as well, saw the nail-pierced body of Jesus as He appeared—wounded and bleeding—when taken from the Cross. Great fear of God and strong conviction fell upon those who witnessed this.

Many similar experiences have occurred in nearly every generation. Wherever our Lord has found a fully yielded vessel, He has been pleased to draw back the veil of the flesh, at times, and permit a few, at least, to see Himself—Himself living in one of His earthen vessels! This sacramentalizing of the house God has given us affords Him the opportunity to manifest Himself openly in wonderful ways. He gave His Body for us, can we do less for Him?

In the Old Testament we find the record of a number of Theophanies, often in the body of an "angel." How wonderful were these appearings! Even more glorious shall be His appearings in the many members of His redeemed Body who have been made "bone of His bone, flesh of His flesh!" Indeed, at the consummation of the age, there shall be a worldwide manifestation of Jesus Christ in the sons of God, who shall go forth to every nation in the Name and image of Jesus, displaying His grace and salvation, and judgment, to the entire earth. For this we wait! For this we pray! For this we prepare! And even now we experience foretastes of that great day!

It is wonderful to behold our Lord in dreams and visions! It is yet more glorious to have our inner eyes opened to see HIM and comprehend HIM in the Spirit. But the day is at hand when we shall behold Him openly, unveiled, revealed in flesh, in very substance! The imagination plays no part in this whatever. It is a supernatural experience in which Christ moves and speaks and works HIS works. This revelation is astounding in effect. No other experience brings us into such heights and depths of insight and suffering, and glory!

"Blessed are the pure in heart for they shall see God." How near He draws to us! "Pleased as man with men to dwell—Jesus, our Immanuel." One poet has written, "It was ever God's way to take man's way with men." If only man would be as willing to take God's way with God! He draws so near that He can speak to us, touch us with His touch of love, comfort us and quicken us—transforming us into His likeness. It seems that His heart is so filled with love for us that He cannot wait for His appointed hour for open manifestation, but comes to us as to those "born out of due season," giving us foretastes of consuming bliss and reality!

"Ah, but this is only for a favored few," some will cry. True! But God favors those who favor Him and seek His favor rather than the approval of men. "The King's favor is as a cloud of the LATTER RAIN!"

Others raise their voices in unbelief, as though this were some new doctrine which had not existed from the beginning, unmindful that many and diverse have been His appearings. Unbelief is forever blind!

But the few, with eager hearts, cry out as those of long ago: "We would *see* Jesus!" And they who behold Him, forevermore shall say: "We would see no man, save Jesus only!" With all the fervour of our grateful hearts, we testify:

"The Lord hath appeared of old unto me, saying, Yea, I have loved thee with an everlasting love: therefore with loving-kindness have I drawn thee." (Jer.31:3)

And the beloved Gospel song rings true:

> "I have SEEN Him, I have KNOWN Him,
> For He deigns to walk with me,
> And the glory of His presence
> Will be mine eternally:
> O the glory of His presence,
> O the beauty of His face,
> I am His, and His forever—
> He has won me, by His grace!

—F.M.

"Behold what manner of love the Father hath bestowed upon us that we should be called the sons of God: therefore the world knoweth us not, because it knew Him not. Beloved, now are we the sons of God, and it doth not yet appear what we shall be: but we know that when He shall appear we shall be like Him for we shall see Him as He is." (1 John 3:1-3)

THE APPEARING OF JESUS

God's waiting people—the people who are expecting and looking for the mighty outpouring of The Holy Spirit in the latter days—are becoming more and more sensitive of a new pulse in spiritual things.

During the long period of preparation they have experienced many things: crucifixion, rest, rapture! Many spheres have been entered and passed; some very dark places reached—and penetrated. There have been exciting and delightful places too, encountered in the exploration for the hidden treasures of God's personality.

But this is something different—something entirely NEW. These heights, now being scaled, are the last spheres—the realms beyond which there is *ne plus ultra*. The realms supernal—eternal; broadening and expanding in revelation and vastness. Eternity is being invaded!

This is the BEGINNING of the APPEARING and REVELATION of JESUS CHRIST! This explains the mighty undercurrent of expectancy... the anticipation, exultation of Spirit... the wonderment. Many, catching the waves of this new spiritual vibration, are making it a great pompous thing, seeking to draw the crowds. Prophecy is made a fetish, and the sensational is exalted, instead of exalting the Lord Jesus Christ.

Not so, with the "hidden-away" saints! The true lovers of God are beholding wonderful things! They are plumbing His secrets, receiving astounding revelations and enlightenment. What's more, they are seeing the Word bear witness of itself in substance.

Heaven and earth are kissing each other... blending. The power, and the rule, and the authority of the Kingdom of Heaven is asserting itself to those who are in the Kingdom, overthrowing the rule of the existing powers of darkness. What a paradox—when it seems that heaven and earth are so far from one another, due to the raging inferno engulfing the world—that God is so present and manifest to His hidden saints.

"Behold the darkness shall cover the earth, and gross darkness the people, but the Lord shall arise on thee and His glory shall be seen upon thee." (Isaiah 60:2)

God is introducing Himself in flesh. He is demonstrating His power and authority and sovereignty in many matters. The flawless perfection of His laws He exhibits and proves. He is moving among us as an humble servant... as a King and as a Man! The revelation of Jesus Christ shall be based upon His humanity as well as on His Divinity! He, the King of Heaven, is coming down among men to set His Kingdom in their midst. He is moving among men as a Man. His favorite name for Himself was "the Son of Man."

This revelation of Jesus Christ may perhaps be quite unexpected to the people who have formed their own concept of how He is to appear. God will never be fettered by the finite thoughts of men. There is only ONE to whom He will condescend, and that one is His dove-like Bride. While those on the outside are talking *about* the Lord, The Bride is in His courts talking *to* the Lord, and to her—lo! He appears!

—L.V.

WHEN JESUS APPEARS

Yes, it is heaven! The state of the soul, on finding its Redeemer, has entered the very realm of God, and is beginning to take its first steps in the heavenlies. Praise the Lord! Is this not a most glorious experience? And each day, as we walk through this new Land, we make new and more amazing discoveries. His heart of love affords us a great Treasury, hitherto unknown to us, a hidden mine, as it were. How thrilling the thought that the mine you have discovered is YOURS for an eternal possession!

True, we are taught by the blessed Holy Spirit to share all things, and to help and instruct one another in that which we have learned of Him, and yet—the Lord deigns to give us the unique satisfaction of possessing Him, ourselves, *individually*, as Saviour, King, and Lord of all! And as the Holy Trinity are in a constant communion of interchanging love, and mutual devotion to One Another, so we learn to love to share our life in Christ with others who have found Him. Jesus has appeared! "Fade, fade each earthly joy; Jesus is mine! Break every tender tie; Jesus is mine!"

Then: living in Him, abiding in Him—we find a place of rest where the soul knows Him better each day. Knows Him in trusting, in obeying, in rejoicing, in love, and in patient suffering.

Interwoven in this lovely pattern of the soul-life is a lovely golden thread, precious in the eyes of God. We speak of the gift—for gift it is—of utter abandonment. This is an unquenchable thirst for Him. It is the desire of the skill of an artist that cannot accept that which is inferior, or imitative. It must have the ultimate! It can find its only satisfaction in God's artistry and in His design! Therefore, what can there be to hinder the lover of God from pouring out his love and adoration to Him? Who should arise to quench the fire that burns in the poet's soul, the poet who sings forth the eulogy of God's name? Why cannot the dancer, because of her soul's delight in her lovely Bridegroom, praise Him in the holy dance of abandon? And how can anyone looking in the eyes of one who finds Jesus in all things—Jesus, the Divine Lover who ravishes her heart—dare to shut from her view the adorable vision?

Oh, let us find this grace of complete abandonment... completely conquered by Christ... Then Jesus can appear in all things. We shall see Him in the most lowly objects... in the most insignificant things as well as in things of moment. When we think of Him consciously or unconsciously every hour of the day and prize His Presence as a divine treasure: then we shall most assuredly give His loving heart joy!

Let us become, as one writer has said, "desperately in love with Jesus Christ." This love makes a life a human torch—the fuel of the flame of God, burning with "heavenly recklessness."

Let us become His pastureland, where He can come to refresh Himself; His temple, wherein His holy vessels lie; His true companion, ready to go with Him into any realm; a joyful troubadour of holy song. Let Jesus appear and be manifest in all things, and say with Job: "I have heard of thee with the hearing of mine ear, but now my eye seeth thee."

And this is the song thy heart shall sing!

> I see Him in the roses,
> > That, trellised o'er my gate,
> With their sweet sister, Daisy
> > Are joyously elate;
> I see Him in the clouds on high,
> > In the sky so clear and blue;
> I hear Him in the singing birds,
> > That trill His love anew;
> The winds in passing, carry
> > His words of love to me,

The trees whisper with their rustling leaves:
    "How wonderful is He."

I see Him in the sunshine,
    The snowfall and the rain,
And in the loudest thunder
    He shouts to me again!
I hear Him in the bustle
    Of a day so filled with care,
Or, cloistered in a silent room,
    I feel His presence there.

I see His face so lovely
    In the dearness of a child;
I find Him in the hearts and hands,
    Of friendships sweet and mild;
I see Him in the spirit
    Of the loved-ones that I meet;
I see Him in the lame, the blind,
    The beggar on the street.
He calls to me from everywhere,
    What else can my heart seek!
When Jesus dear, appears to me,
    And through all things does speak!

                  —C.V.

TO THOSE WHO LOVE HIS APPEARING—
SALUTATIONS!

Lo! He comes!
He comes to me, in you, dear one!
How He loveth to appear in flesh;
He loves to come the humble way, as Son of Man!

Oh, Thou blessed Lord, open wide our eyes that we may see Thee and recognize Thee. Let us care not in whom Thou dost come, so long as we see Thee and honor Thee! And, Dear Lord, give us, we pray Thee, ears to hear Thy voice, no matter through whom Thou dost deign to speak—whether in titled man or aged godly woman; well-known priest or prophet; the stranger within our gates; ragged beggar; or our own kin or spouse; the humble passer-by, or the innocent child—let us hear, heed—and obey only Thee! Thou dost appear in whom Thou wilt—only help us to know Thee, Lord!

Lo! He comes to me in you, and to you and me. A Christ—ALL—and in you all! So doth He reveal a definite phase of His own blessed self in each precious vessel.

Yea, He cometh, soon cometh! He comes to us in each other. Blessed Jesus! Reincarnate in flesh! May you see Him only, always, in me. Yea, and Amen! He is here—in His sons and daughters. No longer do we know one another after the flesh... we discern the Body of our Lord! For have we not seen Him... in His beauty... in His glory... in His majesty!

Yea, and in His suffering and humiliation He hath shown Himself; in His love and compassion; in power and dominion; in might and wonder; in faithfulness and in faith. Yes, by sight we do see Him—for He doth appear to us in flesh! And have not ye all seen

Him? Is it not true that His sons have been crucified with Him and that now He liveth in them? This is the will of the Father.

Yes, we do see Him today in His called and chosen vessels, whom He is forming in His own image. We have seen the King! We glimpse Him now, and we shall see Him in His fulness, revealed in human flesh, even in the sons of God!

Let us beware and watch, that we miss Him not! O pray that our eyes be not holden nor our ears of dull of hearing—for we would SEE JESUS, and HEAR Him—when He comes! Once He walked with two whose eyes were holden, until they constrained Him to abide with them that night... then... O wonderful joy... He was revealed to them in the "breaking of bread!"

"For the grace of God that bringeth salvation hath appeared unto all men, teaching us that, denying ungodliness and worldly lusts, we should live soberly, righteously, and godly in this present world; looking for that blessed hope and THE GLORIOUS APPEARING of the great God and our Saviour Jesus Christ, who gave Himself for us that He might redeem us from all iniquity, and purify unto Himself a peculiar people, zealous of good works." (Titus 2:11-14)

—N.L.

I SEE JESUS IN YOU

I see His hands in your hands,
  And in your face, His face;
I see His smile in your smile—
  He's standing right there—in your place!

In your hands, nail-scars I see;
  These feet bear marks of Calvary;
His sweet compassion shows in you—
  He does for me the things you do!

I hear His voice in your voice;
      His eyes are in your own;
I feel His presence in you—
      Feel His and His alone.

I felt His grace in every word;
      And when you spoke, 'twas He I heard:
The gracious words your lips impart
      Are His—He put them in your heart.

His gentleness is in you;
      His sweetness and His grace;
I see the love and joy of Christ
      Reflected in your face!

O, I would see Jesus in you—
      In the words you say; and the things you do;
Always and only may Jesus I see,
      Revealing Himself through you unto me!

—N.L.

SEEING JESUS

Are you "looking" now for Jesus?
Unto you He may appear—
If you're waiting for His coming
And are drawing very near.

As the "Gardener" Mary saw Him
Though she knew not it was He—
In this very tomb they laid Him,
Taking Him from off the tree.

Blinded eyes of Mary? Surely!
That had He to you appeared,
Would you have known the Master?
Unto her He was most dear.

And the hearts of the two disciples,
Burning as they walked along
With the "Stranger" to Emmaus
Knew Him not 'til He was gone.

Thomas saw Him, yet he doubted,
And the others quaked with fear.
What then would be your reaction
If to you He should appear?

Will you know Him when He comes
To fulfill His Word to you?
Or will you as blinded Mary
Think He is the Gardener too?

Will you think Him just a stranger?
Will you doubt it could be He?
Or will your anointed vision
Know it is the Christ you see?

—M.J.P.

MISCELLANEOUS EXCERPTS

The Golden Candlestick

The following are collected excerpts of various teachings, prophetic words, and poems from the journals, missionary notes and newsletters of the Golden Candlestick—primarily from Frances Metcalfe. Some are in bits and pieces as the original copies are very old and corrupted, making a perfect translation impossible. In fact, some of the mimeographs are no longer extant. Still, I believe in order to be "complete" these collected works would require the inclusion of the following.

—James Maloney

THE LIFE AND DEATH OF THE BELOVED

Read My Gospel with expectancy. When you read with the eyes of My heart, you shall discover treasures of beauty and truth never seen before. Seek for these jewels by meditating upon those portions which I shall quicken for you. Come with Me to My land, and share My human life. Enter into the joys and sorrows of My life upon earth. And as you do this, greater insight shall be given as to the walk and requirements expected of those to whom I give My heart and soul—purity, holiness and perfect love. The more joy you bring to this study, the more fruitful it shall be. Read every word of Mine as though reading it for the first time. Forget previous concepts and let the Holy Spirit open the eyes of your understanding. Read

with your heart, not with your head. Open your heart and exult as
you read. Rejoice also that these writings have been preserved by
the Spirit, and remember that even now I have dear ones who have
been deprived of My Word. So read then with gratitude, joy and
appreciation.

> To view Thy life on earth, Beloved,
> Through the eyes of Thine own heart—
> This is my dream, my dear desire,
> I beg Thee, the needed grace impart;
> To see as Thou didst see,
> To feel as Thou didst feel,
> Each event, each act and each word,
> O my darling Lord!
> Recreate them now anew in me,
> That I may share the mystery
> Of Thy wonderful life,
> And Thy more wonderful death!

Reading the Gospel of St. Matthew "through the eyes of His
Holy heart," has been a blessed experience. As never before I felt
the warmth of His human nature—His love and compassion for the
poor, the oppressed, the sick and troubled and His desire to fulfill
the promised Word in Isaiah: "The Spirit of the Lord God is upon Me:
because the Lord hath anointed Me to preach good tidings unto the
meek: He hath sent Me to bind up the broken-hearted, to proclaim
liberty to the captives and the opening of the prison to them that
are bound; to proclaim the acceptable year of the Lord...!" At times
I felt that I was there, walking among the people who thronged
about Him; at other times I seemed to be in the "inner circle" of
His disciples, close by His side, watching Him lay His blessed hands
on the sick, and hearing the music of His voice as He spoke words

of healing and forgiveness: seeing the expressions on the faces of those who listened, and thrilling with joy as their faces lighted up with the conviction of faith that this Man was indeed the Christ, the long-awaited Messiah. His names, "Jesus" and "Son of Man," touched me in a special way—the names which signify His humanity, and as I read, I would repeat these names again and again.

In my attempt to see through the eyes of Jesus' heart, as I read the Gospels, I saw Jesus as a Man of much action and endless vitality. From the time He entered His public ministry to the day of His death, there were few quiet moments He could call His own. People surrounded Him daily, and His disciples were with Him almost constantly. Night was practically the only time He could be alone in communion with His Father. Yet Jesus never flinched nor failed to meet the endless duties of every day. His agenda was full! His was no mere forty hour week! Streaming multitudes were to be healed; Scribes and Pharisees were to be wisely answered; humble petitioners were to be counseled; little children to be blessed; the disciples to be taught and followers to be addressed. He met each day with grace, wisdom and tranquility. He was always master of every situation. Nothing was too much for Him. Though He sat upon no earthly throne, still He rules as King every day and in every way. Truly He is our example as we endeavor to "reign as kings" in this mortal life.

Viewing the life and death of our Lord Jesus Christ through the eyes of His Holy Heart has been quite an experience—a new one surely. It seems to me, from the very first of the Gospels, that LOVE is the dominating factor—the love of the Father and of the Son. His great compassion for us as lost sinners, and willingness to take on our humanity and die on the Cross for our sins, is simply the great manifestation of His love for us. And all through His three years of ministry we see what He went through because of His love for us. Even in His calling of His disciples, we see His great desire for a return of His love and desire for fellowship. We see His love manifested in His compassion for the sick and afflicted and tormented. We see His love in sharing His authority with His disciples. We see His thoughtfulness and consideration for others and thoughtlessness of self, and His great Shepherd heart. But I feel LOVE reaches its peak in the sixth chapter of John when He gives His great discourse on the Bread of Life and goes into such detail regarding the eating of His flesh and the drinking of His blood, in order that we might know real union and communion—an appropriation and a partaking of His Divine nature. He tells us that only His Holy Spirit can quicken or make these great truths real to us. And surely that is true.

I have been deeply moved upon by the heart-wounds that Jesus received from His own loved and chosen ones. On the night of His betrayal there was Judas, who shared His loving fellowship and then betrayed Him. And Peter, so sure of his love and loyalty to his Beloved Lord and Master, denied Him. In the hour of His great suffering, when He needed them to stand by Him, they ALL forsook Him! Not long before they had declared that they truly believed that He had come from God, but when the test came, their faith was shaken. Unbelief entered their hearts. The Lord impressed the word "believe" to my heart in a very real and deep way and I felt how deeply His heart was wounded with their unbelief. My own unbelieving heart was opened before me. I saw my frettings, my murmurings, my discouragements, my impatience, and much more—all of them revealing that unbelief was still a part of my heart. Love and trust are the solvents for worry and cares. My heart cries out with the man who came to Jesus for the healing of his son, "Lord, I believe; help Thou mine unbelief." Trust and rest!

In reading the Gospels again, there have been many rare and beautiful portions especially quickened to me for meditation and special thought. One, in particular, was in the portion of the woman who anointed Jesus' feet. He said, "You gave Me no kiss, but she from the moment I came in has not ceased (intermittently) to kiss My feet tenderly and caressingly. You did not anoint My head with (cheap, ordinary) oil, but she has anointed My feet with (costly, rare) perfume." (Amplified) Another meditation was that in the Gospels, Jesus, the Son of God, exalts and reveals the Father; while in the Book of Acts, the Holy Spirit exalts and reveals the Son of God. There have been new revelations as we have read these beautiful books through the eyes of Jesus' heart. Made ONE with Christ, has been my special thought.

As I reread the four Gospels again, my heart was stirred to a greater desire to LIVE for Christ more perfectly. Three words stand out prominently: HUMILITY... COMPASSION... KINDNESS. Compassion and kindness, in my mind, have always been synonymous. Not so, according to the dictionary. Kindness is defined as an ACT. Compassion is said to be a THOUGHT or DESIRE to help or take on the cares of another, or to suffer in their stead. God is kindness in perfection. And His mercy endureth forever. Even as He hung from the Cross, Christ prayed for His murderers, promised Paradise to a robber and provided a home for His mother. Hallelujah! What a Savior!

> Love has eyes to see in the dark,
> Love has a heart that understands what it sees;
> Love has a way of knowing, instead of guessing,
> About life and all its mysteries.
> I would look at Your life
> With the eyes of love,
> O Jesus, my darling Lord!
> I will seek to understand
> With my heart and my mind
> Your every act and Word.

The Lord has so lovingly let me feel and see His love for the sinner in this new way of seeing and feeling through His heart and eyes. What Love and Compassion! No words of man can ever tell it! I see the sinner in a new, burning light, and feel the yearning of HIS Heart, even His thirst for them that they might come to repentance and the knowledge of His Love. John 3:16 has taken on a new and deeper meaning to my heart and mind. How intensely the Lord lived in His three years of ministry! It seems every day of His life He felt the intense urgency of pouring out His love, compassion, warning and teaching. To me, every Word He spoke was intense, whether spoken in love or rebuke, to friend or foe. And the intensity of His suffering will never be equaled. I feel a new intensity burning within my own heart like a flame ignited by the intense fire of His Holy Heart.

In meditating on Jesus' acts during this period, there was one that was outstanding to me. It was the act of Jesus forgiving Mary Magdalene. Mary, although a "sinner," had come to Jesus as He sat at meat, and had poured out her heart and her treasure (where our treasure is, there will our heart be also.) Her love carried her out of herself, so that she braved the wrath of the Pharisee and his guests to anoint Jesus. How precious were those tears of love. What comfort and refreshing

[*The remaining portion has been lost—James Maloney*]

Advent 1976

Beloved Worshipers of our Lord,

Once again Advent time is upon us. And our hearts reach out to each of you in fervent love and blessing. We ponder again the great wonder and mystery of The Incarnation of the Almighty God in human flesh. Yes, great is the mystery of God made man, the fullness of the Godhead dwelling in Jesus Christ bodily. "For in Him the whole fulness of Deity (the Godhead), continues to dwell in bodily form—giving complete expression of the divine nature." (Col. 2:9 Amplified) The wonder of God walking and talking among men! The lowly Son of Mary! The adored Son of God! He partook freely of the weakness and suffering of mortal man. Of Him it could well be written: so then He who was immortal, put on mortality. He who was incorruptible, put on an earthly body which would on the cross become corruptible. (2 Cor. 5:21)

"Truly, without controversy, GREAT IS THE MYSTERY OF GODLINESS! God manifested in the flesh, justified in the Spirit, seen of angels, preached unto the nations, believed on in the world, received up into glory." (1 Tim. 3:16) And we all marvel and worship and adore Him at this season in which men celebrate His birth, even though the exact date of it is not known.

We are continuing on in prayer, praise and worship here on our mountain. And we take your prayer requests together to the Throne of Grace. How much we appreciate hearing from you! And now it is at the leading of the Lord that we send to you our latest publication, PERFECTING PRAISE. We pray it may inspire and edify you as it has edified us while we lived through the experience recorded in the booklet.

We have four other booklets which are particularly appropriate to give at this season: TAXES OR TRIBUTE, THE SONG OF THE CENTURIES [*sadly, we have been unable to find an extant copy of this work—James Maloney*]; SONGS OF EPIPHANY; and THE INCARNATION. We shall be glad to mail them to you if you have not received them in the past.

We are so thankful for those of you who are concerned and praying about our health problems. My husband is a little better, praise God! But Marian, my co-worker, and I continue to be in very fiery physical trials. And only by a constant exercise of faith are we able to continue in this ministry. He will take us through victoriously, as we continue to trust and praise Him.

All who are of our Fellowship here join with me in sending you Advent greetings. And Marian sends her special love to each of you.

Most lovingly in Jesus Christ,

Frances Metcalfe

Advent 1977

Beloved worshipers of our Lord,

As we come to you again for a time of sharing, we are moved upon about the humility of our Lord Jesus Christ. We feel to follow Him, taking the lowly place of a servant, a "love-slave" to Jesus, letting Him move in us according to His will. We are led to quote Philippians 2, beginning at verse 4:

"Let each of you esteem and look upon and be concerned for not (merely) his own interests, but also each for the interests of others. Let this same attitude and purpose and (humble) mind be in you which was in Christ Jesus. Let Him be your example in humility—who, although being essentially one with God and in the form of God (possessing the fullness of the attributes which make God God), did not think this equality with God was a thing to be eagerly grasped or retained: but stripped Himself (of all privileges and rightful dignity) so as to assume the guise of a servant (slave), in that He became like men and was born a human being. And after He had appeared in human form He abased and humbled Himself (still further) and carried His obedience to the extreme of death, even the death of the cross!

"Therefore (because He stooped so low) God has highly exalted Him and has freely bestowed on Him the name that is above every name. That in (at) the name of Jesus every knee should (must) bow, in heaven and on earth and under the earth, and that every tongue (frankly and openly) confess and acknowledge that Jesus Christ is Lord, to the glory of God the Father." (Amplified version)

May we come to you in this spirit at this season and share in your interests and concerns. If you have an urgent prayer request, we shall be glad to pray with you about it, as we gather together here on the mountain. We are so grateful for your love and prayers for us and for your letters and offerings. We feel a closeness to all of you and to all the members of the Body of Christ. Truly He is drawing us ever closer together. We are glad to be able to send you the enclosed book, THE KING'S PORTRAIT. And we hope it will be a blessing to you. We have several other booklets that are appropriate for this season: GOD'S ANGELS; THE INCARNATION; TAXES OR TRIBUTE; SONGS OF EPIPHANY; and THE SONG OF THE CENTURIES.

Please do continue to hold us up in prayer. Both Marian and I are being severely tested in our bodies and each moment it is an exercise of faith to continue to carry on. Dwight, my husband, is in much pain with arthritis. But he continues to be as active as possible. He is now teaching a special Bible Class at one of the local churches. He would appreciate your prayers for this.

All the dear ones in our Fellowship join Marian and me in sending you love and blessings at this season and for the New Year just ahead.

Yours in Christ's grace and praise,

Frances S. Metcalfe

Springtime 1979

Beloved in the Lord,

We greet you in the name of our wonderful Resurrected Lord! Our hearts rejoice in the life springing forth after one of our coldest, stormiest winters (with more than 10 feet of snow) here on our mountain. Yet, the earth still heralds the Resurrection! May our hearts and lives bud, blossom and bring forth fruit that will be a delight to Him, as we become more attuned to His "times and seasons."

How thankful we are that our dear Frances listened to the Holy Spirit. Although, at times, she did go out to minister, she felt that it was more important to, "write the vision, make it plain... that he may run that readeth." (Hab. 2:2) And, as Peter, she felt it more profitable to "endeavor that ye may, after my death, have these things always in remembrance." (2 Pet. 1:25) With John, "Keep those things which are written, for the time is at hand." (Rev. 1:36) And "These things we write unto you, that your joy may be full." (1 John 1:4)

In the beginning of Frances' ministry, as she was rapt in the Spirit, and taken into the heavenlies, our Lord told her that she was to WRITE concerning the "Apocalyptic appearing of Jesus Christ to the End-time Church." This she faithfully did, for over 40 years. (We have a number of booklets in print—list available upon request.) those of you who have been on our mailing list for a number of years have found that the message of THE GOLDEN CANDLESTICK is to the Endtime Church—a message of praise and worship; a message of union and communion; and of expecting the appearing of our Beloved Bridegroom-King—that HIS BODY in the earth might manifest, not only the gifts of the Spirit, but His glorious attributes and characteristics, the Fruit of the Spirit. O may we be attuned to His slightest whisper, whether it pertain to TIME or ETERNITY.

Our God transcends earthly "time," but He has taught us to be "timed" with Him. There is much in the Word concerning times and seasons, as well as His great clock in the heavens, which wise men have "read" for centuries. The Holy Spirit instructs us to be attuned to His times, although we realize that He desires us to be aware of the past, present and future—the eternal NOW of God. "Behold NOW is the accepted time, behold NOW is the day of salvation." (2 Cor. 6:2) How we thank Him that He accommodates Himself to our timing also, and speaks to us in words that fit our earthly cycle. "For now is our salvation nearer than when we believed." (Rom.13:22) Praise the Lord!

We thank you for your love-gifts, sent in memory of our beloved Frances, along with words of comfort and encouragement. We look forward to hearing from you, and will be praying for you, and that the enclosed booklet will be a blessing. Please continue to stand in faith and praise for us, as we continue to move in His Spirit.

In His wonderful love,

Marian Pickard, & all the Co-workers of The Golden Candlestick

Springtime 1980

Beloved Saints of the Lord,

"But in the deep dawn of the first day of the week, the women came to the tomb... They were puzzling over this when two men in dazzling robes suddenly took their stand beside them. They said, Why search among the dead for one who lives? He is not here, but is risen, as He said." (Luke 24:1-6) An astounding statement! Made by an Angel of God.

It is fitting that these Heavenly Creatures were present to proclaim His Resurrection—even as they had announced His birth. And later, after His ascension to the Father, angels stood by to proclaim that He would return, "In like manner as ye have seen Him go!" Not only were these angelic beings manifest throughout the Old Testament, and in the life of Christ, but they are spoken of by various writers of the New Testament. And we praise God that He has allowed many of His saints throughout the ages to be visited by His angels. The book of Hebrews tells us why: "Are not all the angels spirits in the service of God whom He sends on His errands for the benefit of those who are going to be unceasing possessors of salvation." (1:14) In these last days we need their assistance as perhaps no generation before us has.

Not only do we expect the visitation of angels, but we are "looking for" and "expecting" the visitation of our glorious Risen Lord. He has promised to "appear to your joy," even as "He showed Himself alive after He suffered death in many convincing demonstrations, appearing to them over a period of forty days, discussing the interests of the Kingdom of God." (Acts 1:3) How we thank Him that He is appearing in these days, teaching, instructing and preparing many for the greater latter-day outpouring that has begun in the earth and will culminate in the mighty Harvest of Ingathering. Signs and wonders are following the ministry of believers, as they did in the early Church, and multitudes are being born into the Kingdom. We praise God for this, as we know you do, and truly believe to see ever increasing manifestations of the Presence and Power of our Lord, in every realm of our lives.

We appreciated your response to our last letter and thank each of you who have sent messages of love, requests for prayer, shared experiences, and sent gifts for the ministry. Our hearts are touched by your love for us, and we are sending the enclosed booklet as a token of our love. May the Holy Spirit make it a special blessing. We look forward to hearing from you again.

Lovingly, in the worship of our Risen Lord,

Marian Pickard
For all of The Golden Candlestick

The remarkable teachings of the
Golden Candlestick begin in Volumes
1 and 2, available now!

Please visit www.answeringthecry.com
for more information!

Printed in Great Britain
by Amazon

83820869R00139